HOW TO
WRITE A
NOVEL

Novels by Nathan Bransford:

Jacob Wonderbar and the Cosmic Space Kapow
Jacob Wonderbar for President of the Universe
Jacob Wonderbar and the Interstellar Time Warp

How To Write a Novel © 2013 by Nathan Bransford
All rights reserved.

Published by Nathan Bransford
www.nathanbransford.com

1st Edition: October, 2013

Cover Design by Mari Sheibley
Interior Design by D. Robert Pease, walkingstickbooks.com

Published in the United States of America

FIRST THINGS FIRST

Rule #1
BELIEVE!

The first thing you need to know about writing a novel is this: you can do it.

No, really. You can. Lesser people than you have written a novel. I'm not saying they were all good, but they did it. You can, too! And if you read this book, and apply the rules and advice herein, it will probably be pretty good!

I spent eight years reading slush as a literary agent at a century-old agency, so I can say this with authority: you can't possibly go and write the worst novel ever written. It's already been done. Don't even try.

You probably shouldn't try to write the best novel ever written either, because the resulting paralysis will turn you into a miserable alcoholic.

Instead, write the novel you want to write. Strive for quality, write something you love, and don't become a brooding, cafe-squatting malcontent that people avoid at parties. You will learn a lot from the writing journey, you will be thankful you have written a novel once you're finished, and humanity may thank *you* for shutting yourself inside long enough to write something that brings meaning and entertainment to the world.

You can do this.

Proof: I did it! I once harbored major doubts about whether I could really write a novel. Then I went and wrote one, and it didn't get published; then, I *really* doubted whether I could write a novel. But I had another idea, I wrote a new novel, I found an agent, and the end result was the *Jacob Wonderbar* series. What's more, I wrote it while maintaining a more-than-full-time job. I didn't even get fired.

If I can do it, you can do it. But you have to want it.

There will come a time in the course of writing a novel where you would rather rip off your toenails and light them on fire than write one more word. This is normal.

There will be days when scrubbing your floor with a toothbrush will start to sound like a good idea if it means you can avoid writing. There will be days when you will contemplate driving yourself to the nearest mental institution and hurling yourself onto the reception desk, because anyone who would devote so much time to writing a novel when the rewards are so uncertain is surely insane.

This is also normal.

This is because writing, when done correctly, is not always fun. If you think writing a novel will be completely fun, you should find another hobby, like playing laser tag on ice skates. Or something. I don't know what non-writers do with their time.

Writing is not always fun. It shouldn't always be fun. You're not doing it because it's always fun.

The only reason to write a novel is because you have some insane fire burning inside that years of therapy have been unable to extinguish, and you fear how disappointed you will be with yourself if you never do it. Or, you know, because you really, really want to do it.

You have to want it. You have to work at it. You have to be able to write when the weather is teasing you with its pleasantness and when your friends are merrily drinking bottomless mimosas without you because they are happy non-writing jerks.

It's hard. It really is. But, again, you can do this.

You, the person who may not always have had the best work ethic. You, the person who wonders whether they're really creative enough to think up enough ideas for a whole novel. You, the person who thinks the whole thing seems magical and impossible.

You, the person with the nagging voice in your head that says, *why do I want to do this again?* You, the person who feels like they never have the time. *You* can write a novel.

And if you've already written a novel, you can learn to write an even better one.

Here's how.

Rule #2

THINK OF AN IDEA YOU LOVE ENOUGH TO NEGLECT EVERYTHING ELSE YOU ENJOY IN LIFE

The first step in writing a novel is deciding what in the heck you're going to write about.

There are many horrible reasons for choosing what you're going to write about, and only one correct reason.

The horrible reasons are almost always variations of one basic and colossal mistake, which is that you are choosing a particular idea because you think it will make you mountains of money.

Visions of endless mahogany bookshelves, of sparkling blingety bling, and of being featured in the *New York Times Book Review* with the headline "Wunderkind" motivates writers to do many ill-advised things, but perhaps the worst is when they cause writers to chase trends. Take this one to heart: if you're chasing a trend (vampires! post-apocalyptic!), you're already too late. (See Rule #7, if you are feeling particularly stubborn on this point.)

Avarice is what motivates people to write in genres they don't particularly like. It pushes them to choose ideas that they don't love enough to make it all the way through the writing of the novel. It's what makes an already difficult process completely impossible.

Let's get this out of the way: you're not going to make mountains of money writing books. You're not. You're really, really not.

Okay. Well. Some of you will make mountains of money, but you're most certainly not going to make mountains of money if you are setting out to try and make mountains of money.

The only reason for choosing something to write about is because you love the crap out of the idea.

When you're choosing an idea for a novel, you're choosing something you are going to be spending more time with than many of your best friends and your most demanding family members. You're choosing an idea that will render your bathing habits irregular and your sanity patchy. You're making a terrifically important decision that will shape the next six months to seventeen years of your life. You have to choose wisely.

In other words, it can't be an idea you merely like.

Liking an idea will get you to page fifty. It will give you an initial burst of enthusiasm— a dawning feeling of "Hemingway's daiquiri, I can do this!"—before you inevitably lose interest, your attention wanders, and you find yourself with an unfinished novel that you feel vaguely embarrassed about.

Liking is not enough.

You have to *love* the idea of your novel. Or if not your plot idea, then your main character, your setting, or some part of your novel that will sustain you through painful bouts of self-doubt and distraction.

How do you get to love?

Well, it's tricky. Here are some ways *not* to choose your idea.

DON'T LISTEN TO WHAT OTHER PEOPLE SAY YOU SHOULD WRITE ABOUT

It has become a fashionable conversational crutch to reward a particularly funny or gruesome anecdote, such a harrowing encounter with baggage claim or an apocalyptic string of bad dates, with the words, "OMG, you should totally write a book about that."

Do not listen to these people. Unless the person telling you to "write a book about that" is a publishing professional, assume the person uttering these words is merely being polite and is not looking out for your best writerly interests.

DO NOT WRITE THE NOVEL YOU THINK YOU SHOULD WRITE

Maybe you grew up in an interesting locale. Maybe you've had a Dickensian biography. Maybe your ability to dress kittens in capes is hailed far and wide.

Set it aside. You're not going to get to your best idea by marking off checklists or by applying an algebraic equation to your life that goes, "I experienced X and it was rather intense, so therefore I will use it as inspiration to write about Y."

That's not to say that your real life can't influence your central idea and the contents of your novel. After all, what is the point of writing a novel if not to settle old grudges by taking veiled swipes at people who have wronged you? But, it's important to stop yourself from chasing after an idea by shaking your biography like a piggy bank to see what shiny things fall out. If this happens naturally, and you love an idea that is based on your own life, then absolutely go for it. Just don't do it out of a sense of obligation or because it is the default choice when you fail to think of something else.

You're not going to find your idea with a formula, and it's not going to be immediately self-evident. It has to come to you.

DO NOT TRY TO THINK OF AN IDEA SO UNBELIEVABLY ORIGINAL IT HAS NEVER EVEN REMOTELY BEEN THOUGHT OF BEFORE

I get it. You don't want to imitate. You want to chart new ground and be the most brilliantly original new-thinking writer the literature world has ever seen.

Good luck.

Sure, maybe you're a once-in-a-generation visionary who can conceive of whole genres that have somehow eluded the billions of people who have lived on this planet before you.

But you're probably not. No offense.

Besides, even if completely new ideas weren't logistically borderline impossible, they are also highly overrated. There were wizard schools before *Harry Potter*. There were mystical lands before *The Lord of the Rings*. There were helicopters with dorky names before *Fifty Shades of Grey*.

You don't need to chase the trends that are already out there, but neither do you need a completely off-the-wall and unheard-of new idea that will astound everyone you meet. You *do* need a unique spin and a unique world that are completely yours.

Just don't paralyze yourself by trying to break every mold.

So how do you get to the right idea?

By listening to yourself. By keeping the thought in the back of your head that you're waiting for a really good idea for a novel. By eavesdropping on the people around you to see what inspires you. By letting your mind wander in the shower. By silently thinking, night and day, that you want to write a novel and that you are merely waiting for the right idea.

As you do this, you're priming your brain for inspiration. You're opening yourself up to the world so that the right plot hook or character will flow into you. With every insight you have and every life realization you make, ask yourself: Could this make a novel? Is there something here?

And 99.9% of the time the answer will be, "No, you idiot, that would make a horrendous novel."

Keep asking. You only need that answer to be "yes" just once.

Along the way, you will likely have many false starts and hollow loves. You might not find your idea on the first try. You might start and stop writing a few novels, and you'll start to wonder if you have commitment issues.

Don't worry. This is not evidence of your inability to write a novel any more than that apocalyptic string of dates was evidence that you are unfit for marriage. You just have to keep at it.

When you do find the right idea, you'll know it. You'll just know. It will beat you over the head with its rightness and make you feel like you're skipping through a tulip field while hugging a puppy, because you will have finally found an idea you love enough to turn into a novel.

You may still wonder whether you have enough talent, whether you can really do it, whether you can find the time or whether you will ever get anyone to read it, but your faith in your novel will be unshake-able. And then you can get started writing it.

Does this process sound daunting? Well, buckle up, champ. This was the easy part.

Rule #3
FIND THE WRITING STYLE THAT WORKS FOR YOU

I've always been fascinated by other writers' creative processes. When I first decided I wanted to be a writer, I studied. I observed. I felt that if only I could divine some common thread in the creative lives of the writers I admired, I would then be able to emulate these individuals and be as good as they were.

Going to an Ivy League school and marrying a psychopath worked for Fitzgerald, but should I do that?

Volunteering for wars in exotic locales worked for Hemingway, but should I do that?

Drinking and drugging themselves into oblivion worked for most of the writers of the Western canon

... but do I really have to do that?

Even apart from biography, I delved into the writing process itself. Did they lock themselves in a room? Did they outline? Did they write stream of consciousness?

How did they do it?

Then, after college, I had the good fortune of working for a literary agency, where I had the opportunity to closely observe the habits of some incredibly successful writers, many of whom I had admired since childhood.

And I discovered this: there is no single way to write a novel. There's not much of a common thread that links great writers. The only thing they have in common is that they somehow, at the end of the day, find a way to get the words onto the page.

Yes, this may seem like odd wisdom in a book that claims to tell you how to write a novel, but it's true. There isn't one way to write a novel. There isn't a formula.

Now, before you scurry for a refund and write a nasty review, please trust that this guide will most definitely help to steer you in the right direction. I will help you avoid the pitfalls, and I will help you channel your innate tree-killing thirst, you ritual destroyer of trees at the altar of books.

But *you* have to figure out how you write best.

Po Bronson writes in a closet. Hemingway wrote standing up. Vikram Seth once told me he traveled to

India and intentionally stayed on U.S. time because the disorientation of jet lag helped his creativity.

Are you an outliner? Are you a seat-of-the-pantser? Do you need peace and quiet? Noise? Do you need to write in a cafe? Would you rather work in a closet? Do you want to write on a computer? A typewriter? Pen and ink? Do you want to write quickly and revise a thousand times? Write a near-perfect first draft slowly? Do you want to write every day? Only on weekends? Do you want to stay up late and burn through fifty pages? Do you want to write during the daylight hours and agonize over five words at a time?

It's all completely up to you. There are no common threads shared by great writers other than hard work and talent.

Even the ages at which authors become awesome varies tremendously. Some start young and flame out. Some people arrive at writing late. Some start young and work at it for years before achieving a breakthrough.

I hope you are absorbing the enormous freedom presented in this chapter. Let me say it again: there is no single way to write a novel. You don't have to be constrained by the styles of other people. Don't let other writers get in your head, and don't let anyone tell you that you're doing it wrong.

You don't have to force yourself to outline if you don't want to. You don't have to write every day. (You hear me? You don't have to write every day. I certainly don't.) You don't have to love every moment of writing. You don't have to find it all agonizing drudgery, either.

You just have to be yourself and find what works for you.

All that being said, it is beneficial to be aware of what kind of writer you are because it will allow you to develop a writing rhythm, which will help you feel normal and comfortable, and it will help you to better enforce this rhythm when your attention starts to wander. Whatever style you adopt, you must be diligent and productive.

While everyone is different, every writer falls somewhere on the spectrum between total planners and total improvisers.

The planners outline, plot everything in advance, choose their words carefully, and tend to write a little slow. They go into the writing process with a pretty clear idea of where they're going. But when they're finished, they usually (but not always) have less revision time waiting for them.

The improvisers go in blind, let their instincts guide them, move through quickly, and might not even know where their novel is going until page fifty. They write and write and write until they find the story, and the mere notion of planning everything would stunt their creativity. When they're finished with a draft, they usually (but not always) have a lot of work to do, as they must go back, rewrite everything, and stitch it all back together.

A lot of people are somewhere in the middle. And everyone is doing just fine.

So if you're a planner, just know that it's okay if you move slowly. It's okay that you feel as if you're plodding along, even if your improviser friends have written whole novels while taking a bath.

If you're an improviser, just know that it's okay if you don't know exactly where things are going all the time. It's okay to write in terrific bursts of energy and just get it all on the page, even if it doesn't all make sense or fit together at first. You can trust that you'll figure it all out.

Don't let other people control your writing style or make you feel inferior because of the way you go about it.

As long as you're getting words on the page, you're doing just fine.

Rule #4
FLESH OUT A VAGUE IDEA BEFORE YOU START

As much as it may disappoint us, entire plots do not spring forth fully formed from our brains for us to breezily channel into words. You will not have a Eureka moment where you suddenly have an entire idea for a novel, from start to finish, that you can transcribe in mere days, and even if this should miraculously happen to you once, you should not tell another writer because they will hate you forever.

More likely, you'll have a vague idea that might be the merest embryo of a novel. A tiny shard. A little novel sapling that needs to be lovingly coaxed not just into a tree but into an entire forest.

The entire *Jacob Wonderbar* series emanated from a single idea I once had when I was feeling very relaxed. (Incidentally, the last relaxing moment you will experience is the moment before you figure out what you're going to write your novel about. This is the life you've chosen.)

Here is the idea: a kid gets stuck on a planet full of substitute teachers.

That's it. That's all I had.

When I thought about that kid running away from the substitutes on a strange world, I knew I was going to write the novel. It was that unshakeable needle sticking in my brain. I just had to figure out what in the world was going to happen to fill out the rest of the story—which ended up being three novels.

I had to flesh out the idea.

And yes, all you improvisers out there, this chapter is starting to sound like planning in advance, and you have likely already broken out in hives. But bear with me. Even if you're an improviser, following these few steps will go a long way toward helping you flesh out an initial idea, and this process will give you some surer footing before you start.

Here's how you do it:

1] ASK QUESTIONS

Let's look back to the then-unnamed kid stuck on a planet full of substitute teachers. Here are some of the questions I asked:

- How did he get into space to begin with? (Answer: he traded a corndog for a spaceship).
- Why is he stuck in space? (Answer: when he blasted off into space, he accidentally broke the universe, and now he can't get home).
- Why are substitute teachers in space? (Answer: there's an entire galaxy full of wacky space humans).
- Did this kid really go to space by himself? (Answer: no way, a twelve-year-old would bring his best friends with him.)
- Who are his best friends? (Answer: a sassy tomboy and a timid sidekick who the protagonist is always getting into trouble.)
- Well, where did *they* go if the kid is stuck on the planet by himself? (Answer: they got split up along the way.)
- Who split them up? (Answer: a rogue space pirate.)

And as they say in *The King and I*, "Et cetera, et cetera, et cetera."

The more questions I answered while brainstorming, the more I began to flesh out and add flavor to the world of the novel. These questions aren't just about deciding what actually happens in the plot (much of that can and will change later, anyway). Instead, you'll begin to get a sense of what *type* of novel you're going to write. Is it a funny novel? A sad one? Is it dark? Is it for kids? Adults? You're learning about the setting of the novel, the style of the writing, and where the story is eventually going to go.

Instead of setting out ahead of time to write a particular type of novel, I let the idea guide me. When I had that first glimmer of an idea for *Jacob Wonderbar,* I had no prior notion that I wanted to write a wacky middle grade novel. I just went with the idea. When I started fleshing it out, it sounded like it was for 8- to 12-year-olds, so okay. I had the beginning of a middle grade novel.

Ask questions until your idea starts to make sense and you know what you have. The more you know about your world, the more you can build around your central idea and let it guide you.

2] START THINKING ABOUT WHAT YOUR CHARACTERS CARE ABOUT

Don't stop with questions. Think about what *matters* in your novel.

A secondary idea I had while brainstorming for *Jacob Wonderbar* was that his dad could perhaps be lost in space. It would be too easy if Jacob knew for certain that his dad was out in space, so I created a mystery around it: Is his dad wandering around somewhere in outer space, or did he really just move to Milwaukee when Jacob's parents got divorced?

With every character I introduced, I tried to figure out at least two things they wanted, preferably the type of things where I could put a "but" in the middle when I described them because they don't easily go together. The space pirate loves pulling off wild stunts, but he also wants to be president of the universe. Sarah, the sassy tomboy, cares about her friends, but she also wants to be tough. Dexter, the timid sidekick, wants to stay out of trouble, but he's also loyal to Jacob.

For the novel as a whole, I raised the stakes for everyone: space humans might just want to destroy Earth.

Again, not all of this has to be figured out before you start. It's okay to go in with unanswered questions, but starting to think through the motivations of the characters will help you to guide the story.

3) PUT OBSTACLES IN THEIR WAY

Once I knew that Jacob wanted to find out what happened to his dad, I created one huge obstacle and one huge thing he cared about: he didn't know where his dad was (obstacle), but he really wanted to find him (the thing he cares about).

And oh yes, there is that pesky obstacle of having broken the universe, so it's not easy to get home.

Don't just think about how to get your characters from Point A to Point B as you flesh out your idea, but think about how to make this journey as difficult for them as possible.

With just these initial questions, a few big obstacles, and the underlying motivations of the main characters, I had the basic arc of the entire first novel, and the groundwork for the series, before I started writing.

Jacob trades a corndog for a spaceship and blasts off into space with his best friends. They break the universe (obstacle), they get separated by a rogue space pirate (obstacle), and Jacob eventually begins to suspect his dad is in outer space (obstacle + what he cares about), but he also wants to get back home (another thing he cares about, which competes with his desire to find his dad).

This still wasn't enough material for an entire novel, and there was a ton I didn't know about the story and the characters before I started. However, I had a rough idea of where things were going to go, and I was well on my way.

If you ask yourself these questions and begin to figure out what your characters want, why it all matters, and why their task is difficult, you will be on your way, too.

Rule #5
KNOW YOUR GENRE

It often pains authors to have to shoehorn them-selves into a genre. It seems like an unfair constraint cooked up in some foreboding tower by a cackling publisher, who maniacally decreed one day that authors everywhere must sort themselves into cat-egories before being allowed to enter the gates.

And sure, if you've let your idea guide your novel rather than setting out to write in a particular genre, you may end up with a book that combines a little of this and a little of that until you find yourself with a vampiric unicorn novel set in a technologically advanced future, leaving you with absolutely no idea whether it's fantasy, paranormal, science fiction, or horror. I saw many projects when I was an agent that felt like genre alphabet soup.

But it's not just agents and publishers who care about genre, and these distinctions aren't arbitrary. Who else cares? Readers.

Walk into a bookstore. You'll see that sections are arranged by genre. Go to Amazon or BN.com. The sections are arranged by genre.

These sections don't exist for the health of Amazon or bookstores, nor as a means to torture authors. They exist because readers often know what they are looking for ahead of time and are browsing for something in particular. They are looking for genres.

It's thus very important to know where your novel will sit on the shelf (or virtual shelf), and it's helpful to figure this out relatively early in the process.

Here's why. Some genre readers have expectations for length and subject matter that you may want to take into account in the beginning stages of your novel lest you end up with a novel that is too short, too long, or otherwise offends the "rules" of its genre. If you are writing a novel with particular standards for length and plot contrivances (such as those in science fiction and romance), it is rather helpful to know these ahead of time. Romance in particular has a whole slew of subcategories and organizational rules that you should research heavily before you start.

Even if you're planning to bend some genre rules and break new ground, it helps to know the genre conventions, and thus your reader's expectations, ahead of time, so that you can break these rules to maximum effect.

Perhaps the greatest example of convention breaking is George R.R. Martin's *A Game of Thrones*. Martin knew the fantasy genre backwards and forwards, which for decades had been dominated by hero stories and redemptive plotlines, such as a dishonored knight who saves his realm or a young boy who finds out he has secret powers and defeats the evil bad guy. Martin took those conventions, upended them, shocked his readers, and then he did it again. And again. And again. It was quite thrilling. But you have to know these conventions in order to break them.

It's totally fine to blur genres, and many successful novels do this, but even if you do some mixing, it's extremely helpful to have a base. You can have a fantasy novel with science fiction elements or a literary novel that utilizes a horror plot, but whatever approach you choose should fit squarely in one genre even if it branches into another. This way, it will not only rest comfortably on the right shelf in the bookstore, but it will also be easier to market the book to the hardcore readers of a particular genre. These readers will be the evangelists who will help spread the word to a broader audience.

So yes, it's not romantic to be forced to think about genres and genre conventions before you've really gotten going, but a bit of thought and preparation will help save you from the heartache and the time-consuming revisions that stem from writing a book without a category.

FORMAT YOUR WORK PROPERLY FROM THE START AND, FOR HEAVEN'S SAKE, BACK IT UP

It may seem highly premature to talk about formatting here, as this is only the sixth chapter in this guide to writing a whole freaking novel, but getting your formatting correct from the start will save you from the tremendous annoyance of having to clean up 250 pages of incorrect tabs and spacing issues.

It is up to you which word processing program you wish to write in, but whatever you do, make sure you can export your document to a Microsoft Word–compatible format.

Why? Because this is what agents and publishers will expect you to send. I'm writing these words in 2013, but this advice will probably still hold true in 2063 when you consider that people in the publishing industry were still sending manuscripts around on floppy disks in the early 2000s (yes, really).

Here's how to format your work:

- Double-spaced
- 1" margins
- 1/2 indent for a new paragraph
- Numbered pages (and make sure that the page numbers don't restart with every new chapter)
- Page break after the end of each chapter
- No fiddling with anything else. No messing with the spacing between paragraphs, no widening the type, no full justification, and no hyphenation. Basically, just open up Word or an equivalent app, hit double-spacing, make sure the pages are numbered, and start typing.
- Most important of all, do not, and I mean do not, try to format your manuscript to match the layout of a book (or if you do, change it back before you send it to anyone).

That's it. As long as you follow these basic formatting steps, you'll be fine.

If you want to get more granular, for chapter titles I hit the return button twice, center the chapter title, hit return twice again, and then start with the first paragraph. This provides a bit of a visual break without needlessly padding the page count with a ton of space at the top. One space after periods.

Also, before you begin, come up with a plan to back up your work. Do it now and stick to it. Personally, I would rather step on a rusty nail than re-write something I've already slogged through once.

By the time you read this, the technical possibilities for saving and storing your work will have changed from the time I'm writing it, so very wondrous are the world's computer geeks, who invent new whiz-bang things every twenty minutes. But whatever method you choose, it must pass my ironclad "What if I got robbed on the way home to my burning apartment???" test.

Let's say you are sipping a latte and tap tap tapping away on your computer in a cafe. You save your work, you leave the hipsters behind, and then you are accosted on the way home by gremlins who steal your laptop and simultaneously set fire to your apartment. (Why? They're gremlins! Who can say why they do what they do?)

If your backup system depends solely on your laptop's hard drive and/or a backup drive at home, guess what? You no longer have a manuscript. The gremlins have won.

To be more realistic, let's say you go out on a Trader Joe's run and your house either burns down or is robbed by very thorough thieves, costing you both your laptop and your backup drive. You may have delicious taquitos, but you no longer have a novel.

Instead, take advantage of the computing cloud. E-mail your manuscript to yourself all the time. Use a storage site like Dropbox. Sync everything to iCloud or write in Google Docs. Save to thumb drives and secretly bury them under rocks in local parks. I don't care. Just don't let the gremlins get you. Make sure that if you lose your computer and your home backup drive, you won't lose your novel.

And if you write by paper and pen . . . well, God help you. Avoid gusts of wind and sudden downpours.

Rule #7
DON'T CHASE TRENDS—I MEAN IT: DON'T DO IT

One of the most popular pastimes at writers' conferences, and at any gathering where more than one writer or publishing type is present, is to discuss the latest trends in the book business.

People want to know which genres are hot, which are not, and which unjustifiably popular writers should be arrested by the book police. Of course, agents and editors will dutifully answer the "What's hot?" question when they're asked, as they want to appear as if they know what in the heck they are doing.

But here's the thing about "what's hot/what's not" trends: they're completely pointless for writers to think about.

Let's say, for instance, that you looked at Publishers Marketplace today and saw that lots and lots of books have been sold that feature monkeys. Monkey fiction, monkey nonfiction, monkey memoir (my favorite), or monkey romance. You go to a writers' conference and hear an agent say, "I'm looking for historical fiction, narrative nonfiction . . . oh, and monkeys are really hot at the moment, so if you have a great monkey book, come and talk to me."

You naturally start thinking to yourself, "Hey! I should write a book about monkeys!"

So you sit down to write the book. A year later, you have a finished and polished monkey novel.

Then you try to find an agent, and this takes six months. Then your agent sends your manuscript around to publishers, and this takes another couple of months. Then your book comes out a year after it sells to a publisher.

That's *three years* from when you first heard that monkeys were hot. At best, it would be one year if you decided to just cut to the monkey chase and self-publish.

That's one to three years for people to get really, really tired of monkeys. One to three years for that whole monkey thing to totally crash and burn. And, wouldn't you know it, by the time your book comes out, monkeys are, like, so totally over, and everyone wants books about narwhals.

If you try and write your book according to trends, you're playing a very risky game. The industry and reading public will likely have moved on to the next thing by the time you've even completed your manuscript. Trends move fast.

If you want to glom on to a hot trend, here's your one and only strategy: be lucky.

All those people who looked as if they hopped onto the zeitgeist at just the right time weren't psychics. They didn't capitalize on their ability to divine what would be popular two years from the time they started writing. No. They got lucky.

I'm serious! Ask them! They wrote something they loved, it was good, it got published, and it just happened to be what readers wanted at that exact time.

Don't worry about the fads and don't follow the trends. Be original. Write what you love. It's better to start a trend than to chase one.

Rule #8
DON'T BE A CLICHÉ

So. You're avoiding trends and are striving for originality. Good, but . . . let's make this a bit more complicated.

Here's the thing about originality: it is somewhat, but not completely, overrated.

Everyone wants to be original and think of totally new stuff that blows people's minds. And yes, again, don't just go and write in whatever genre is popular at the moment. But if you actually stop and think of your favorite stories, chances are they're not really all that original.

There are many, many stories involving a young man, often of unknown/mysterious parentage, who suddenly realizes he's the chosen one and has to embark on a quest against impossible odds to save his people.

Yet *Star Wars*, *Harry Potter*, *The Lord of the Rings*, David and Goliath, *Eragon*, and countless other stories are all different and much beloved.

There are many, many stories involving a girl who meets a mysterious/scandalous/acerbic man who she falls in love with even though she probably shouldn't, and often only after he tells her she shouldn't. Yet *Twilight*, *Pride and Prejudice*, *Jane Eyre*, *Fifty Shades of Grey*, and countless other stories are all different and beloved.

There's an old adage that there are really only six to a dozen different stories (the number always changes). These are archetypes, and we've been telling variations of these stories since the days when we recounted myths around campfires and painted them on cave walls.

You don't have to be wholly original. You really don't.

At the same time, there's a very fine line between embracing an archetype and writing a cliché. We've all read stories that feel tired and worn. Whenever an author is employing an archetype, they run the risk of the reader rolling their eyes and saying, "Yeah, I've read this before." Archetypes, when handled incorrectly, can become predictable and fall into the dark pit of cliché.

So how do authors navigate between archetypes and clichés?

By telling a familiar story differently. By making their version stand apart from all the others.

Now for the tricky part: doing it differently is much harder than it seems.

There's a mistaken belief that to set the millionth take on an archetype apart from all the rest, all you need to do is just give it a little twist.

It's like *Twilight*, only with zombies! Voila!

It's like *Star Wars,* only the Dark Side wins! Voila!

It's like *The Road,* only people don't eat each other! Voila!

That's not the way it works. It's not a matter of coming up with a twist or two and otherwise appropriating a previously created world. That's when projects fall into Cliché Canyon.

Here's what you have to do instead: you have to tell a familiar story in an entirely new location, and the story has to have its own rules, its own unique characters, and it has to be told in a unique style.

This is why we have stories as varied as *Star Wars* and *Harry Potter*, even though the basic arcs of the stories are similar. The settings, characters, style, voice, and secret powers could not be more different.

This is why no one confuses *Pride and Prejudice* with *Fifty Shades of Grey*, even though the male foils are vaguely similar. The scope, style, and worlds would never be confused.

It's not enough to start a story with a boy who has to save the realm/galaxy/kingdom from disaster. What's different about this setting, this character, and your particular style?

It's not enough to start a story with a woman who, while personally quite modest, somehow attracts the attention of every man within a forty-mile radius, especially the handsome and mysterious rogue who she (gasp) most certainly should *not* be attracted to (oh my).

What sets this woman and man apart from the rest? What is it about your characters, your world, and your style that is truly yours? This may primarily seem like a concern for genre fiction, but it goes for literary fiction, too. It's important to be cognizant of the elements that set your novel apart from the rest, even if you're re-telling an old story.

It's okay to use an archetype as long as you aren't letting other takes on this archetype seep into your novel and as long as the key elements in your novel are original.

The road to cliché is paved with imitation. Start fresh.

Rule #9
YOU HAVE TO HAVE A PLOT. AN ACTUAL PLOT.

Now you have an idea for a book, and it is mos def not a cliché. But do you have a plot?

Multiple choice quiz (hope you did your homework!):

Which of these is a plot?

a) Four women find redemption and love on a trip to Italy.

b) A young man comes of age in an unpronounce-able kingdom.

c) A man and his video game collection discover the true meaning of love.

d) Three friends on a dinner cruise realize they totally hate each other.

The answer: none of the above!

These are not plots. They are themes, the undercurrent of meaning that happens beneath the surface of a novel. Coming of age, triumphing over adversity, and defeating personal demons are all ways of describing the inner journeys of characters. Themes, essentially, are what a novel is *about*.

"It's about this guy who discovers the meaning of life!"

"It captures what it's like to be young and single in the big city!"

"It's sort of hard to explain, but it's about how this depressed penguin regains his sense of purpose!"

All these statements describe why the events of the novel are meaningful to the character, but they're not plots.

Plot is not what a novel is about. A plot is what *happens*.

So let's try that again. Spot the plot in these:

a) Snakes get loose on a plane.
b) A cat with a hat arrives to entertain children.
c) A crazy man hides out in the jungle.
d) The world is going to end when the Mayan calendar runs out in 2012. (Because the Mayans were right about *everything*. Also, we're still alive.)

Which one is the plot?

Also none of the above. (Don't hate me. I trick because I love.)

These are not plots; they are hooks! Or premises! Or whichever label you prefer!

A hook or a premise is a starting place. It's the first important thing that happens in a novel that sets the story on its way. A premise is just that: a premise, a place where something starts. But a starting place is not a plot. Where does the novel go from there?

Enough with the trickery. What really makes a plot?

Think of a book as a really big door, preferably one of those Parisian ones that are thick and heavy and last hundreds of years. Here's how the different parts of a novel break down.

Bullet-point time:

- The premise is what happens to knock the door ajar. Something jolts the protagonist's life out of balance. Preferably something that is really intriguing, life-changing, or, like, totally deep, man.
- The climax is when the door closes: maybe the protagonist makes it through the door; maybe the protagonist doesn't make it through the door, but he or she learns a really great lesson about door closing; or maybe the door chops the protagonist in half.

- The theme refers to how the person who opens the door changes along the way.

So what's the plot? Plot consists of an event that sets the protagonist's life ajar and a big obstacle/complication that prevents them from setting things right. It is the premise plus a major complication that tests the protagonist. It's what opens the door, but it is also what keeps the door from being closed.

premise + complication = plot

Not quite visualizing it? Check out these examples:

- *Gilead*: An aging man writes a letter to his young son (premise) because he doesn't think he'll live long enough for his son to really know him (complication). (Also, don't you want to cry already?)
- *The Invention of Hugo Cabret*: A young orphan in Paris wants to repair an automaton because he thinks it will give him a letter from his deceased father (premise—also, more tears), but in order to do so, he must avoid the Station Inspector and enlist the help of a mysterious toy-store owner (complication).
- *Harry Potter*: A mildly acerbic child finds out he is secretly a wizard (premise), but a monstrous individual who cannot be named wants him Avada Kedavra'd (complication).

A good plot starts with an interesting premise and an interesting door-block. There is something big standing in the way of the protagonist closing the door.

A *great* plot also forces the protagonist to start out on a long quest (either internal or external), which is what makes the reader want to read more. We want to see a character go on an interesting journey, and we want to see the ways in which they change after facing great obstacles along the way. This does not have to be a physical journey. It can also be an emotional journey, such as trying to find a wife, achieving a very difficult task, or overcoming personal demons.

There are precisely five components to a good plot, and you need them all:

- Something happens to set your protagonist's life ajar
- He or she wants something really big
- He or she goes on a physical or mental journey (or both) to try and get that thing
- He or she encounters obstacles of increasing intensity along the way and experiences up and down moments in pursuit of that thing
- He or she either does or doesn't get that thing but ends up irrevocably changed

I didn't invent this; Aristotle did. It's called an Aristotelian Arc. Luckily, he's dead, so he can't sue me.

When you're starting a novel, don't just think of a theme or a premise and leave it at that. The complications and obstacles are everything. Send your protagonist on a quest and put a bunch of huge obstacles in the way.

The complications are, in fact, the plot. Make sure you have them.

Rule #10

EVEN IF YOU'RE WRITING LITERARY FICTION OR MEMOIR, YOU STILL NEED A PLOT

Those who are writing literary fiction or memoirs may roll their eyes at some of the examples cited in this guide to writing a novel, which tend to skew toward science fiction, fantasy, and other genre-ish stories for the simple reason that these are often easier examples to illustrate.

And to be sure, there are important differences between literary fiction and memoir, on the one side, and genre fiction on the other.

But please don't cast out this advice as a result! Unless you're writing something that is wholly experimental and non-narrative, the fundamentals in this guide very much apply to literary fiction and memoir. You still need a plot. You still need conflict. You still need a climax. In fact, you still need virtually all the elements you read about in this guide. The nuts and bolts may be hidden by the style you bring to the table as a literary writer, but the underlying structure should still be there.

There are two main differences between literary fiction and genre fiction that are important to understand:

1) IN GENRE FICTION, THE PLOT TENDS TO HAPPEN ABOVE THE SURFACE, WHILE IN LITERARY FICTION THE PLOT TENDS TO HAPPEN BENEATH THE SURFACE

Whereas the plots in genre novels usually involve things happening in the physical world (chases, shoot-outs, battles, love scenes, etc.), in literary fiction the plot often happens beneath the surface, in the minds and hearts of the characters (decisions, moments of understanding, meaningful interactions, etc.).

Elements of the plot may indeed happen on the surface, particularly in genre/literary hybrids, but the things that are really important are the thoughts, desires, and motivations of the characters, as well as the underlying social and cultural threads that act upon them. The plot may be buried to such a degree that, if you had to describe the book in a short sentence, it could seem plotless, but this simply means that the plot points relate to the inner mind rather than to a chase or a lightsaber battle. The climaxes and nadirs may be hidden in quiet moments and small but powerful revelations.

Even when the prose is straightforward, literary fiction is often more challenging to read than genre fiction because it requires the reader to infer a great deal of the plot rather than to simply sit back and watch the plot unfold. It requires empathy to relate to characters as human beings, to deduce the hidden motivations and desires that lurk beneath their actions, and to grasp how important these motivations and desires are to the characters. The reader has to recognize the small turning points, the low points, and the high points based on what they know about the characters and about human nature.

There's a reason why very few literary novels end with a shootout (er, except for *The House of Sand and Fog*). What happens out in the world isn't as important in literary novels as what happens within the minds of the characters, and thus the climax might be something as small as a decision or a new conviction.

47

But make no mistake, these decisions and turning points, and these highs and lows, constitute a plot, and they are just as important in literary fiction as they are in genre fiction.

2] STYLE AND PROSE ARE EXTREMELY IMPORTANT IN LITERARY FICTION

What ultimately makes literary fiction literary is the style of the author's writing. Literary authors have distinct, polished prose, and that authorial voice is what sets literary fiction apart from genre fiction. The prose elevates the novels into something approaching art, even when a literary novel has a genre-ish plot.

Literary writers have an extra requirement: they must demonstrate a unique style. However, all the fundamental principles in this guide still apply, whether it be voice, setting, organization, or the principles of writing good dialogue.

So too with memoir. One of the most difficult challenges a memoirist faces is shoehorning one's life into a narrative arc, but this is absolutely necessary.

It's not enough to just recount a chronology and to tell it well. Readers expect a story. They expect that the author will start in one place and end in another, will change along the way, and that the character will experience highs and lows.

In other words, they expect the same types of

things from the narrator of a memoir as they do from the protagonist of a novel.

Yes, make sure the events are true (or composited where necessary), but also make sure that the memoir ultimately reads like a novel.

So buck up, literary writers and memoirists. Everything in this guide goes for you, too.

Rule #11
DON'T TRY TO IMAGINE YOUR WHOLE NOVEL ALL AT ONCE

I've given you some weighty things to think about.

Archetypes! Clichés! Plots! The inseparability of plot from literary fiction!

You may be feeling some brain fatigue, and you may have started wondering if this whole writing racket is way more complicated than it's worth. (Note: it is, but I can't stop you now).

Let's zoom out for a moment and remember that writing a novel *is* extremely complicated. So complicated, in fact, that you cannot possibly hold your entire novel in your head all at once. And that's okay.

If you try and imagine your entire novel all at once, and attempt to consider it in its entirety with all of its various ins and outs, your brain will suddenly become so heavy that you will topple over backwards and pass out.

Don't become intimidated by the bigness of the task. It's huge. It's really, really gigantically huge. That's okay. Don't let it overwhelm you.

The best thing you can do is to break the novel up into comprehensible components that you can think about in a coherent fashion, set the rest aside for a moment, and try as hard as you can not to be intimidated by all the things you're not thinking about.

That's what this writing guide is for. You don't have to think about everything—about conflict, about perspective, about plots versus archetypes, about the inseparability of character and plot, and about . . . dear God, what did Anne Lamott say again?—while you're writing. It's impossible to remember everything you need to do at any one time.

Instead, think of this guide as a checklist. Make sure you're doing these things at some point in the writing process. Account for them in your plan. Keep in mind that you do need to make sure you have a plot, you do need to make sure that your characters are doing interesting things, and you do need to make sure you have more than just a theme. But you don't have to do all these things all at once.

Just go back and check off the list periodically. Once it's checked off, you won't have to worry about it anymore, at least until you go to check on that writing element again (and tick it off the list again).

At some point, you have to block out all the weighty nuts and bolts that go into writing a novel and just write. Plow ahead and trust that you'll get it all sorted out eventually. Don't get lost in the weeds and let all the things you have to remember paralyze you and keep you from writing.

Just bear them in mind and charge ahead. When you're stuck, come back to this guide and look at your novel again to see if you've gone astray or if there's something else that you can fix, and keep doing this until you solve the problem.

Above all, don't think you always have to know exactly what you're doing. I rarely do.

Rule #12
YOU HAVE TO START SOMEWHERE

So, uh, how *do* you get started writing a novel?

Start writing!

Kidding. Kind of.

One mistake that often deters people from writing the novel they most fervently desire to write is that they're intimidated by how large the task can loom. They freeze up at the mere thought of writing and discover how much fun housework is in comparison to sitting down and confronting the hugeness of writing a novel. Or they stall, attempting to think through every single aspect of the book before actually putting fingers to keys.

There's a reason for this: writing a novel is hard. It's easy to get intimidated, but the real trick is to avoid thinking you need to have everything figured out before you start writing.

J.K. Rowling and J.R.R. Tolkien and H.G. Wells and J.D. Salinger and George R.R. Martin and every other initialed or non-initialed writer out there did not wake up one day having magically conceived of every spade of grass, every glass of butterbeer, every creature in Middle Earth, and every stone at Hogwarts.

You don't have to have everything figured out before you begin. Don't feel like you have to know precisely how the whole novel is going to work before you get started. There's plenty of time for details later.

When you're just starting to write a novel, there are only two things you're looking to find: voice and plot.

That's it! Two things. You can totally wrap your head around two things.

And all the world building, all the ins and outs, and all the "how in the heck am I going to make this work?" You can worry about that as you go along. Voice and plot are what you're looking for when you start the actual writing.

How do you find your voice and your plot?

Well, if you are a planner, you can craft an outline that can help you figure out your plot in advance. I lean toward the planning side of the spectrum, and while I don't know everything that is going to happen,

I have some major points I want to hit on the way. If you're an improviser, you can write your way to your plot, and you won't need to know exactly what is going to happen right off the bat. Just get going.

Planning and improvising are the two basic ways to find your plot, but there's only one way to find your voice: start writing, and keep writing until you find it.

When you're looking for your voice, don't worry about polish. Don't fret if the first chapter comes out horribly. Don't worry if it feels like you're imitating another writer's voice at first. You're going to revise these first pages so much that they'll be completely unrecognizable by the time you're done with your novel anyway, so don't get bogged down trying to perfect them.

Just get words on the page. Keep going. Your voice may come to you instantly, it may take fifty pages, or it may take several years. Just keep at it. Push through. Stretch yourself and try different things.

Write your way to your voice.

At some indeterminate point, when you have been at it for a while, you'll hit a magical flow and realize you have found your voice. All of a sudden you'll have it, and it will just feel right. It will feel like it's coming from *you* and not from the novels you've read in the past.

Once you find your voice and plot, you can always go back and revise what you've written to make sure everything is consistent, organized, and harmonious. You'll have plenty of time to trim and refine the parts where you were hunting for plot and voice in the mystical land of "I Have No Idea What I'm Doing."

Start writing. It's time. You're ready. You have nothing to lose and a whole new world waiting for you.

PEN TO PAPER
(OR FINGERS TO KEYBOARD)

Rule #13
WRITE A KILLER FIRST PAGE

The first page is perhaps the most important part of your entire novel.

Prospective agents will read the first page and decide whether they want to keep reading or not. Prospective editors will read the first page and decide whether they are engaged enough to consider acquiring the book. And then, most importantly, prospective readers will thumb open your novel, start reading the first page, and decide whether they want to buy it or not. Which is to say, there are a lot of gatekeepers and stakeholders who will develop a powerful first impression based on the way you begin your novel, and this will heavily influence how many people actually end up reading the whole thing.

No pressure, though.

The thing is, you probably already know this and have internalized it. You've heard all the advice about how important it is to grab the reader right away. You have your own personal experience to draw upon, where you have made countless reading decisions based on how a novel opened. You know perfectly well, and have already lost sleep over the knowledge, that your opening has to be good, thankyouverymuch. And as a direct result of this, 90% or more of the first pages I saw as a literary agent failed for one reason: they tried too hard.

Yes, your beginning is important. Yes, it's important to grab a reader right away. But this doesn't mean you have to grab the reader by the throat and start punching them in the face. The first page doesn't have to be the world's largest fireworks show.

Trying to do too much with your first page is a serious danger, and in fact, I'd argue that "grabbing the reader" is entirely the wrong way to think about a first page.

Here's what the first page needs to do: it needs to establish the tone and voice of the novel, it needs to get the reader into the flow of the book, and it needs to establish trust between the author and the reader.

That's it. That's all you need to accomplish with the first page. You don't need to have pyrotechnics, and in fact, even if you *do* have pyrotechnics, you still have to accomplish these three things.

Nathan Bransford

Once more with feeling. A first page has to:

- Establish tone and voice
- Get the reader into the flow of the novel
- Build trust with the reader

You don't have to set up some elaborate high-concept hook, you don't have to cram the entire plot into the novel right away, and you don't have to try to blow the reader's mind with your cleverness. A first page doesn't have to be the apex of genius and breathless ambition. Just start easing the reader into the world of the novel.

Another way to think about it: the first page is like starting a dance with a reader who can't hear the music. You have to ease them in and guide them until they find your rhythm.

Still another way to think about it: the reader has been blindfolded and dropped into a world they can't see. You have to explain what's in front of them.

As you begin, you're establishing a flow. One thing leads to the next, which leads to the next, which leads to the next. You're drawing a reader in. You're giving them a chance to establish their bearings and giving them confidence that you know where you're going.

It's hard to begin reading a book. The reader is starting with a completely blank slate and doesn't have any context for understanding what is happening or where they are. It takes a lot of brainpower to read an opening, figure out what's going on based on the initial descriptions, and begin to feel comfortable in the world of the book. It's very easy to feel disoriented or disengaged and then to give up entirely.

So even if the novel begins with action, or *especially* if it begins with action, it's very important to draw the reader in methodically, with one thought leading to the next, giving enough description and grounding detail that the reader can orient themselves, but not so much that they get bogged down. The flow of the words and a steady build go a long way toward hooking the reader. Anything that jumps around needlessly or feels scattered will make it difficult for the reader to stay engaged.

As you work to build that bond with your reader, it's crucial to shy away from anything that feels like a gimmick, which undermines the trust you're trying to build. Using a gimmick in the opening is kind of like shaking the reader's hand while wearing a hand buzzer. They'll never trust you again.

In general, be wary of anything that feels forced: forced cleverness, forced wordiness, forced cheekiness, forced sagacity . . . anything that doesn't feel natural and authentic. Great first pages feel effortless, but of course these are anything but effortless.

As you think of how to start, you may want to avoid these common openings. I'm not saying they can't be done, but I literally saw hundreds of variations of these openings during my time as an agent:

1] A CHARACTER WAKING UP

Sure, there's probably a good reason why the character is waking up. Maybe their house is on fire, they're late to school, or they just realized their insides are being sucked out by a sea monster. But not only is waking up overdone, what exactly is gained by showing a character wake up? Why not just cut to the insides-getting-sucked-out chase?

2] A CHARACTER LOOKING IN A MIRROR

I know what you're thinking: "How in the heck am I going to show the reader what this character looks like when it's a first person narrative? Hmm . . . a mirror!" Don't do it. Find another way.

3] EXTENDED DIALOGUE WITH INSUFFICIENT GROUNDING DETAIL

It's difficult for readers to be dropped into a new world and get their bearings. It's even more difficult to feel grounded when two characters are talking and you're not really sure who they are or what they're talking about.

4] ACTION WITH INSUFFICIENT GROUNDING

It's really difficult to care about what is happening in an action sequence before the reader knows where they are and why they should care. Make sure there's enough establishing detail for the reader to sort out what's really happening.

5) CHARACTER DOES SOMETHING ROUTINE, BUT OH BY THE WAY THEY'RE DEAD

By all means, tip off your reader that they're dealing with an undead protagonist, but playing it for shock value probably isn't going to work. Think about it. By the time the reader picks up your book in the paranormal section of the bookstore, with the title *Being Dead Sucks* and a cover to match, are they really going to be surprised when your protagonist does something and then you pithily reveal that they're dead?

As usual with writing advice, it's easier to describe what you shouldn't do than what you should do. Remember that you don't have to perfect your first page on the first try. There's plenty of time to get it right later.

The most important thing you can do over the course of writing and re-writing your first page is to have faith in your own ability and to trust the reader to recognize it.

Don't try too hard. Or rather, do everything you can to hide your immense effort.

Rule #14
GET PERSPECTIVE

Before you decide which perspective you're going to write your novel in (and you should know conclusively as you're writing), let's get the definitions out of the way. Here are the four basic perspectives of novel writing:

- **First person**: Told from a narrator's perspective. "I did this, I did that."
- **Second person**: Written as if the narrative happens from the reader's perspective. "You did this, you did that." (Don't write a novel this way. Seriously. Don't do it.)
- **Third person limited**: The narrative is tied to one character's thoughts and perspective at a time. If the perspective shifts, it is almost as if the camera

is handed to another character. "He did this, she did that, but he wasn't sure why she did what she did."

- **Third person omniscient**: This is almost like a god's-eye perspective. Sometimes with the omniscient perspective there is an all-seeing narrator who is almost another character, while at other times it is simply a dispassionate voice describing thoughts and actions. "He did this, she did that, he was thinking this, she was thinking that."

There are also two main temporal choices:

- **Present tense**: Told as if it's happening right now. "He thinks, he does this."
- **Past tense**: Told as if it happened sometime in the past. "He thought, he did that."

Sometimes novels contain multiple narrative styles, but unless you're going for something extremely experimental, if there's a switch to a new perspective or tense it should be contained within its own chapter. It's okay to shift the perspective to another character within a novel, but it's extremely difficult to do this within a chapter without bewildering the reader.

You may be entering the novel writing process with a strong preference for which perspective you wish to employ, in which case you should sigh in relief because choosing whether to write in first or third or limited or omniscient or past or present can be tricky.

The absolutely most important initial fact to keep in mind as you're deciding between perspectives is to remember the constraints of a first person narrative: every single thing that happens in a first person narrative has to be filtered through the narrator. Your reader only knows what your narrator knows. Your reader only sees what your narrator sees. The only things you can show on the page are the things the narrator learns, and they can usually only be shown at the time that the narrator learns them.

Nothing happens for the reader in a first person narrative unless the narrator knows about it. It's trickier than you might think to pull this off.

In a first person narrative, it's really hard to show the reader things that are happening "offstage" that the narrator doesn't know about. You can't show the enemies plotting the downfall of your first person narrator. You can't show the person hiding upstairs waiting to kill your first person narrator. For that matter, your first person narrator can't die without some massive literary theatrics.

And you have to shift the plot accordingly. You have to engineer the plot so that the narrator learns what the reader needs to know at key moments, and you have to construct the entire novel around the things the protagonist actually sees, learns, and experiences.

Not only that, but in the case of the first person perspective, everything has to be filtered through the lens of the narrator's personality. Things don't just happen in a first person narrative, as we see them through the narrator's singular perspective. This can be enormously challenging, but on the plus side, it can be a fantastic way of seeing the world through someone else's eyes. So there's that.

Some really compelling first person narrators give their take on something that is happening, yet it's clear to the reader from clues in the narrative that it's not the whole story. These are unreliable narrators, such as Nick Carraway from *The Great Gatsby*, Tyler Durden from *Fight Club*, or Lorelei Lee from *Gentlemen Prefer Blondes*. They tell their tales in such a style that there's a creeping sense that there's more to what they're telling you.

Other first person narrators may be reliable but have a hilarious, incisive, or chilling perspective on the world, like Bridget Jones from *Bridget Jones' Diary*, Ishmael from *Moby-Dick,* or Humbert Humbert from *Lolita.*

The reader knows they're getting a biased or singular look at the world, which is why it's often so fun to read a first person narrative. We're seeing the world in a completely new way. We start to know these first person narrators better than they know themselves, so much so that we can sense what's lurking beneath the surface of the narration.

The other massively important thing to consider about a first person narrative is that the narrator has to be compelling and likable. Why? Because nothing kills a first person narrative quicker than an annoying narrator. When only one person is doing the vast majority of the talking, this voice needs to be tolerable, but even better, it should be appealing.

Now, this doesn't mean the narrator has to be a good person. They don't always have to do the right thing, and in fact they can do things that may be abhorrent, but they have to be compelling. They have to pass the "stuck in an elevator" test, which goes like this: Would you want to be stuck in an elevator with this person for six hours? Would this person gradually drive you crazy with their annoying habits and tics? Would you be disgusted by their presence? Or would you be so fascinated after being stuck with them for six hours that you would then beg them to grab a cup of coffee with you?

It has to be the latter. The character can be a disgusting affront to humanity provided they are a *compelling* disgusting affront to humanity. (More on this in Rule #22.)

Now for third person.

There are many different ways to craft a third person narrative, and perhaps the hardest part is deciding how far you want to get inside your characters' heads.

Do you want to use that God-like ability to really show the reader every single thought? Or do you want to keep their thoughts slightly hidden? Do you want to stick closely to one character at a time (third person limited), or do you want to keep things more like a bird's-eye view (third person omniscient)?

I tend to believe the most interesting third person narratives leave some distance between what is happening and what the characters are thinking. These narratives get inside people's heads, but not *too* far. They might show specific reactions in specific moments, but we don't see every single thought. There will be times when we see the characters do things, but we won't know the precise reasons, which means that we have to infer for ourselves what was motivating them.

This way, if the reader does not know every single thought, the reader must work to empathize with the character and understand what they are feeling in that moment based on the character's actions, but their heart will remain somewhat hidden. We may see what a character does, but we have to decide for ourselves why they're doing it. The author will tell us enough to get a sense of the character's motivation but without spelling out, at all times, every thought that goes through the character's head.

For instance, in *The Love Affairs of Nathaniel P.* (written in third person limited), Adelle Waldman is able to make plain that Nate is unable to properly communicate his true wants and desires to his girlfriends, but only the reader, and not Nate, sees that he is driven by a mix of conflict avoidance and a heightened self-regard for his own post-feminist enlightened outlook on the world. In great third person narratives, it feels as if we know the characters better than they know themselves.

As with first person, the reader will still wonder about the gap between what he or she sees on the page and what's really happening in the world of the novel. The reader will wonder about what's really driving the characters. But in the best third person narratives, we're piecing together motivations and feelings based on what the character is doing rather than being told every single thought that the character has. We get glimpses into their heads, but their heart will remain partially out of view. It's sort of like looking into a well-lit house from the street.

Also, keep in mind that some of the plot constraints of first person also apply to third person limited; namely, the reader only knows what the anchor character knows, which can necessitate some plot theatrics. In the *Harry Potter* novels, which is a strict third person limited narrative tied very closely to Harry, the author, J.K. Rowling, used the pensieve (a device that transports a character to show them the past) and the invisibility cloak (exactly what it sounds like) in creative ways to show Harry things he wouldn't otherwise have been in a position to see.

So how do you choose your perspective?

Partly, you have to consider the demands of your plot and whether you want or need to be able to show certain things that can't be seen by your protagonist. This could push you to third person by default.

However, it's more likely that you'll find the right perspective by testing them out. Try writing the same scene in first person, third person limited, and third person omniscient and see which one you prefer. Try telling it from three or four different characters' perspectives and see which one feels the most natural and which one you like the most. Keep experimenting with different approaches. One will definitely feel like the right option, and you'll gradually find your novel's voice.

Then you can really get started.

Rule #15
DON'T GET TOO ATTACHED

From the moment I placed the final period at the end of the last sentence of my first published novel, *Jacob Wonderbar and the Cosmic Space Kapow*, I imagined the beginning of the sequel starting in a very particular way.

It was unexpected! Shocking! A little bit unsettling!

But after I submitted a partial draft of the beginning of *Jacob Wonderbar for President of the Universe* to my editor, she came back and said (very politely), "The opening doesn't work."

"What?!" I sputtered. No way. I went to my agent. Could this be true? Could the opening really not work?

My agent (very politely) agreed with my editor.

GAH!

But . . . but . . . I wanted to say, this is how I always imagined it! It's part of the fabric of the novel. How can I write this novel if this isn't the beginning? This *is* the novel. This is how it starts. If it doesn't start this way, I don't have a novel.

Then, after much reflection, I took a step back and realized something: they were totally right. It didn't work! Not even a little! I had been wrong all along.

Thankfully, these trained publishing professionals saved me from one of the deadliest foes a writer can face: the first idea.

First ideas are much like first loves. You fall hard for someone, they become your everything, and you love them to the point of rendering yourself completely bonkers. You can't imagine life without them.

Then there's a calamitous breakup, and you think the world is quite possibly going to explode, but after some time passes, you realize that the person was perhaps quite nice, but you know what? They kind of smelled funny and they weren't really the be-all-and-end-all, and maybe I should have wondered about that collection of ninja throwing stars *before* I found one stuck ominously in the dashboard of my car.

Um. Where was I? Oh yes! First ideas.

The point is this: first ideas have a tendency to become intertwined with your conception of the novel. You start to think: This is how this character *is*. This is how this world *is*. This is how this novel *is*. If this thing doesn't work, well, I guess the whole thing isn't going to work, so phooey patooey.

Some writers say you have to think of ten bad ideas for every good one, while others say you should discard five *good* ideas for every one you keep.

The one thing all this advice has in common is the notion that no idea is sacred. If it doesn't work, it doesn't work. Never become so wedded to an idea that you ignore your doubts about it. Don't get too attached to any one element, character, or idea.

It's important to move past these first ideas and avoid having them become too intertwined with how you envision the entire project. You shouldn't change a novel beyond the point where it stops being the story you want to tell, but short of this point, every single thing in the novel is changeable.

Becoming overly tied to one approach is extremely dangerous if you start ignoring those niggling doubts about certain elements of the novel because you feel as if you simply can't part with those first ideas. You can go down some very dark roads due to your inflexibility. That first idea becomes an iceberg that can sink your whole novel.

The thing is, who owns these characters? Who owns this world? Who tells everyone in the novel what to do?

Spoiler: you do! You're the writer. You can change it to make it work. You really can. You are the master of your characters and plot and setting. They do not own you. Everyone has to do what you say, I promise.

I always find it curious to hear authors who are so completely in thrall to their worlds and characters that they describe themselves as being powerless to decide what a character will do next. "Well, I thought my novel was going to be one way, but dag nabbit, that Joe Joseph character had other ideas."

And I start wondering, "Wait a second, who's in charge here?"

Once the characters and worlds begin to feel lifelike, it can be dangerous to let the characters take the story in a completely different direction. Willful characters can walk themselves straight out of a plot if the author loses touch with the story and instead just follows the characters' whims. These whims, it must be said, are actually the author's whims, because the characters are not real people. You are writing a BOOK.

Yes, listen to the inner logic of your characters and adjust your course if the path you originally chose for them no longer makes sense. But remember, there is nothing sacred about the ideas you have for these characters or their motivations. You are not transcribing real-life events in an alternate universe, as much as it may begin to feel this way. Don't become beholden to the paths the characters initially take.

Take a throwing star to your first ideas. Your second or tenth or hundredth idea is bound to be better. Just remember who's in charge.

Rule #16
GIVE YOUR CHAPTERS DRIVE

Too many writers treat their chapters like a tank of gas. They take off without really knowing where they're going, drive around aimlessly until they run out of fuel, sputter to a stop, and then they start the next chapter after someone takes pity on them and tows them somewhere new.

This is the wrong way to go about it.

Think of a well-constructed chapter as a mini-novel. It has a beginning, middle, and end. It builds to a climax. It transitions toward the next chapter, as if the entire novel is a series of mini-novels.

In other words, chapters are the building blocks of novels, and constructing them well is something writers don't often think enough about. Would you build a house with misshapen and poorly constructed bricks? I dare say you wouldn't!

Chapters can be as long as one hundred pages or as short as one page, depending on your style and genre. Most books tend to have chapter lengths that are relatively consistent, which helps maintain a somewhat uniform pace, but there's nothing to stop you from changing things up if it's warranted.

A chapter should start off with an open question, meaning the character(s) at the heart of the chapter has something that he or she is trying to accomplish. Is the character trying to find the bad guy? Convince their love interest to kiss them? Survive a day at school?

Then they encounter obstacles, and things steadily get more intense before culminating in an exciting, intense, or thought-provoking climax, whether it's the resolution of a gun battle, a profound moment that passes between characters, or even a somewhat quiet realization that the character reaches independently.

The highest or lowest points of most chapters shouldn't have the intensity of the nadir or apex that your novel's climax represents, but the chapter climax should at least be the most important point within the chapter itself.

If the most important event in a chapter happens in the middle, you may leave the reader wondering what happened to the momentum. If the chapter doesn't end in a compelling place, your reader may not want to start the next one. If the chapter wanders around aimlessly without building toward something, your reader might start losing interest.

If you know what the most important moment in the chapter will be, you can build toward it. Keep it in mind as you construct the rest of the chapter and steadily ratchet up the tension, thinking about what obstacles you can introduce as that moment approaches. Being cognizant of this organization will help give your chapter a shape as you move the reader steadily through the events.

If you don't know what's going to happen before you start writing a chapter, just get it all out there. Take the tank-of-gas approach and write until you've exhausted everything that could possibly happen in the chapter. But then, once you're done, re-read the chapter, see where the most important event occurred, consider combining different elements into one important moment, and then reconstruct the events so that the important event is as close to the end of the chapter as possible. Then layer in the motivations, obstacles, and desires.

If you can't think of a way to reorder the events, or if there are multiple important moments, consider inserting a chapter break in the middle and making it two chapters.

Chapter breaks are one of the most versatile tools in your writing arsenal. They can punctuate the climax of a scene. They can be used to change the scenery or skip over unimportant events. The next chapter can begin in the next instant after the last one finishes, or it can pick up hundreds of years later. You can use these breaks to create unbearable tension or to give the readers a breather.

And, importantly, you can also use them to create a cliffhanger.

The key to crafting a great cliffhanger is to construct the climax of a chapter so that its resolution opens up even bigger questions. Think about the fate of Dumbledore in the *Harry Potter* novels, Han Solo being frozen in carbonite in *Star Wars*, or "Who shot J.R." on *Dallas*.

If you think about the great cliffhangers in narrative history, they're always about dangling an important question and making the reader wait for the answer. Dan Brown uses these to great effect in *The Da Vinci Code*, which has a breakneck pace that is propelled in part by the way he uses chapter breaks to leave questions unanswered until the next chapter. The chapter break heightens the mystery and builds suspense by forcing the reader to wait a bit and then re-engage with the narrative before the answer is revealed.

Chapter breaks are magical. You have to use them wisely.

Like this.

Rule #17
IDENTIFY YOUR TENTPOLES

Hopefully by now it's clear that novels aren't simply a collection of random events that somehow all come together in the end. Some writers have an intuitive grasp of narrative arc and are able to create good structures without even knowing they're doing it, while other writers need to be more systematic and scientific in how they approach it.

There are some writing gurus who will tell you to write five-act books like Shakespearean plays, there are some who will tell you to write three-act books or seven-act books, and there are some who will tell you to follow some other type of rigid formula that will culminate in a perfectly organized climax that closes all the narrative arcs.

I do not write like this. Not by a long shot. But I do have tentpoles.

As the metaphor implies, the tentpoles are the events that prop the novel up like a circus tent and give the narrative arc its steepest and most dramatic peaks and valleys.

These are the major turning points, where characters either get split up or are rejoined, where people have heated fights, where the most dramatic mysteries are revealed, and where the most exciting action scenes take place. These are the payoff moments, where the conflict and action you've steadily been building for several chapters come to a head.

I like to think of the tentpoles as points of no return, where characters make decisions or are placed in situations from which there is no easy recovery. These points of no return don't necessarily imply that the events are literally irreversible, just that when your reader reaches one of these points in the story, it should feel like stuff just got *real*.

For instance, I built *Jacob Wonderbar and the Cosmic Space Kapow* around the following five tentpoles (spoilers):

The kids blast off into space and break the universe (point of no return: they can't get home).

Mick Cracken jettisons Jacob and Dexter onto a planet that smells like burp breath, while Sarah decides to help Mick steal a giant diamond (point of no return: Jacob and Dexter are separated from Sarah, and Jacob would be mad at Sarah if he knew what she was up to).

Jacob and Dexter argue, and Jacob is captured by wacky scientists (point of no return: the kids are now completely split up).

Sarah and Dexter are reunited, and they help save Jacob from a band of angry substitute teachers (point of no return: they're now reunited, but they quickly begin to argue about whether to go back to Earth).

After talking with the King of Everything, Jacob ultimately decides to postpone his search for his possibly-lost-in-space father, and the children go home (novel climax).

How many tentpoles do you need? It's up to you. I usually aim to have three big turning points planned before I start writing, including the climax, but I'll inevitably figure out some more as I go along.

Once you know these moments, you can think of ways to make them as dramatic as possible by weaving together your different plot threads. Raise the stakes for the characters in these moments. If the characters need to split up, think of ways to make it an acrimonious or a bittersweet split, and then plant the seeds for this conflict in the preceding chapters. If it's appropriate to the genre, think of ways to punctuate these scenes with action or romance. Once you know which way the big events are going to go, it's much easier to build toward them in interesting ways.

Whatever your approach, your novel has to have a structure. Once you have your tentpoles figured out, your novel will have the shape it needs.

Rule #18
SHOW PERSONALITY

When we think of especially memorable characters, there are often key details that stick out in our
minds: Ron Weasley's red hair, Jay Gatsby calling
Nick "Old Sport," and Ahab's wooden leg.

There's a reason for this. The best way of showing
a character's personality is through detail. It's crucial
to weave in these small moments and attributes that
allow us to fully imagine the character as if they're a
real person.

As you're fleshing out a character, here are some
different ways to show a character's personality
through key details. Once you know these, you'll be
able to weave them into the narrative.

STYLE AND TASTE

What clothes does the character wear? Are they messy or spotless? Do they wear scuffed shoes or do they peg their jeans? Is their hair a wild mess or immaculately groomed?

How do they decorate their bedroom? Do they have posters on the wall or naval maps? Is everything in its place or is everything a disaster? Do they even have a bedroom?

Who are their favorite bands, their favorite authors, and what are their favorite movies? How do they spend their spare time? Do they go skateboarding in the park or do they find a quiet place in the library?

Imagine the character going through their day. After they wake up, what's the first thing they do? Take them through an entire routine day.

As you're writing, look around at the things that surround you. Then, think about what your characters would own.

GESTURE

Emotions are universal. We all experience sadness, surprise, love, hate, annoyance, affection, excitement, boredom, etc. However, the manner in which we react to these feelings is totally unique. Some of us react to anger by lashing out, while some of us hold it in. Some of us react to surprise by freaking out, while some of us laugh our heads off. As you show characters reacting to feelings, there is an enormous opportunity to avoid telling the reader what your character is feeling and instead show that emotion through gesture. Your character's reactions will help make them unique.

How does your character react when they're bored? Do they tap their foot, silently seethe, find a hair on their arm and pluck it, or have a meltdown?

How do they react when they're happy? Do they jump in the air, shout Woowee!, or slump their shoulders and say that something bad is around the corner?

Characters don't always react consistently to emotions, but if you have a general sense of how they respond to common emotions, you'll be able to show the reader who they are.

WORDS

No two characters speak the same way. The manner in which characters choose to express themselves reveals a great deal about their personalities. This is not only about showing a regional accent (and more about that in Rule #28), but also about showing how a character interacts with the world.

In general, are they boisterous and excitable or careful and reserved? Are they outgoing or quiet?

How do they break bad news? Do they come right out with it in a rush? Are they careful and compassionate or brash and careless?

What do they do when they're backed into a corner? Do they try to lie their way out? Apologize and try to make right? Distract people from the issue at hand?

Characters should never say exactly what they're thinking. Instead, showing how they express their thoughts and emotions will reveal a huge amount about them.

HOPES AND FEARS

Ultimately, the true measure of a character is what lies in their hearts. What are the things that your character wants and fears the most? Characters' decisions are perhaps the most crucial way of showing what truly makes a character tick and what they really care about.

Which is why I devoted the next chapter to motivation.

MAKE SURE YOUR CHARACTERS ARE MOTIVATED

Motivation.

This is the powerful emotion that inspires people to get off the couch and grab a tub of ice cream. It's the only thing that is strong enough to pull me out of a very warm bed when it's still dark and cold outside. It's what inspires Harry Potter to defeat Voldemort in *Harry Potter*, Elizabeth Gilbert to find food, meaning, and companionship respectively in *Eat Pray Love*, and Frodo Baggins to make the long walk to Mordor in *The Lord of the Rings*.

Every good book begins with a protagonist who wants something. There's a reason you don't generally see books about characters cast about by the whims of fate without any sense of purpose or desire, or, worse, characters who are aimlessly wandering about trying to *find* their purpose. Even Odysseus, essentially a powerless character blown about by the gods, has a rock-solid motivation: he wants to get home.

Wanting something is what makes protagonists interesting. It's what makes readers invested in finding out if the character is going to get the things that he or she wants. It's what makes these characters feel like living, breathing humans. After all, we all want something at any given moment.

Your character does not have to know what he or she wants on page one, but it should be conclusively clear by page 30, preferably earlier. Every step that your protagonist takes after this point should be a step toward this goal, though the forward progress will be thwarted by obstacles and other characters, who have their own set of desires and motivations.

Many stories, especially genre novels, have a built-in motivation that's kicked off at the beginning, like a parent whose child was kidnapped or a save-the-princess fantasy novel. The character's motivation is immediately apparent based on the situation they find themselves in.

Better yet is a novel where a character wants more than one thing and these two things are at odds. The main character might want to save the princess, but he might just have his eye on the king's throne as well, and so he has to decide by the end of the novel which of these two motivations are more important to him.

Better still is a character that wants things that are internally contradictory, so that the character not only has to battle exterior obstacles to get what he or she wants, but the character also has to battle their own conflicting desires.

Here's a way of illustrating that in *A Game of Thrones* style.

- Good: Ned Stark wants to help his friend, King Robert, protect the realm.
- Better: Ned Stark wants to help his friend, King Robert, while also protecting his family.
- Best: Ned Stark wants to help his friend, King Robert, while also protecting his family and maintaining his personal sense of honor, but he may only be able to do one of the three.

When I was crafting the plot of *Jacob Wonderbar and the Cosmic Space Kapow*, it was important to me that Jacob should have competing desires in the climax. He isn't just trying to figure out how to get home to Earth, as he isn't even sure if he *wants* to go home. He isn't sure at all about what to do in the end.

Before the climax, I steadily built up the idea that perhaps Jacob's dad was in outer space. Jacob could continue looking for his dad in space or he could return home with his friends, but he couldn't do both. He had to overcome his own internal battles to make this choice. He had contradictory motivations.

The desires of your characters will help shape these crucial choices in your novel. Every time you introduce something a character wants, either internal or external—regardless of whether they want to save a princess, seek acceptance from their parents, or snare a white whale—you're introducing a plot arc.

A plot arc is basically a drawn-out process in which a character wants something and then tries to get it. The arc closes when they succeed or fail in getting what they want.

Every single character you introduce, major or minor, from your protagonist to the pizza delivery robot, should have their own plot arc(s) with defined goals and motivations.

If you're a planner, write these arcs down and know them by heart. Map them out from beginning to end. You should be able to create a spreadsheet of everyone's arcs, which are shaped by the things they want and their high points and low points as they try to get them.

If you're an improviser, make sure that when you're finished with your draft, you can trace these arcs from start to finish. Look for moments when characters don't display enough motivation, and consider rearranging some events to make the arcs fit together more cohesively.

The more important the character, the longer and more complex the plot arc(s). For instance, your main protagonist's and your main villain's plot arcs should be introduced early in the novel, and you will probably have a rather nuanced view of their desires and contradictions.

We probably don't need to know about the existential crises of the pizza delivery robot, but it should still show some sort of motivation if it is to be an interesting character.

Motivation is often where writers miss opportunities. Their characters seem flat because there's nothing beating in their hearts. A character without motivation is an automaton. They're just going through the motions.

Instead, at every step of the way, on every page, with every exchange of dialogue and every action, the best characters are actively trying to achieve their desires. Every character is motivated. Always ask yourself what they want. Then construct obstacles, whether internal, external, or both, that stand in their way. They're encountering characters or monsters or inanimate barriers that want something different than they do and that are stopping them from getting what they want.

This is conflict. More on that in a jiffy.

Rule #20
EMBRACE CONFLICT

You often hear writing advice that stipulates that you need conflict everywhere in a book. Writing gurus say you need it on every page, from start to finish, in every scene, nay, in every passage of dialogue, nay, in every word, nay, in every letter.

Pshaw, says I. *Pshaw.*

Sometimes a character just needs to stare at the ice floes and contemplate the meaning of life and other great imponderables, like how people serving coffee are called baristas and people serving alcohol are called bartenders, but what do you call them when they serve both coffee and alcohol? (I'll give you a moment.)

Great novels have stretches where there's not a hint of conflict and things are serene and beautifully written, and I'll never urge a writer to rip these out to introduce a gun battle.

But make no mistake: conflict *is* essential. It's a book's oxygen. It gives it life.

In fact, let us count the ways that this conflict/oxygen metaphor is apropos:

- Your book needs conflict to survive. It doesn't need it constantly, but a book without conflict is pretty much DOA. It's not really a novel without conflict. It's just some paper with words printed on it.
- If any stretch of your book goes too long without conflict, your reader will die of boredom.
- You can use a lot of conflict to create a bright flame of a book that is relentless and charged, or you can create a slow burn that is more muted but intense nonetheless. You can vary the degree of conflict within the same book to do the same thing.

With regard to this last point, some might say that thrillers and other genre novels tend to put a lot of conflict on the page, and the conflict comes fast and intense, whereas literary fiction tends to have less conflict.

As a very rough and general rule this may be so, but it's not always the case. When you look at Ian McEwan's books, for instance, especially *Enduring Love,* nearly every exchange and moment on the page is intensely filled with conflict. The characters are constantly in conflict with each other and with themselves, and it's a very intense reading experience as a result. And there are plenty of suspense novels where things build slowly and steadily and where the quiet moments contribute to the sense of dread.

There are two main types of conflict in a novel:

- There's conflict that happens on the surface, demonstrated through the actions and thoughts of the characters.
- There's conflict beneath the surface, which is implied and unsaid.

For instance, a gun battle or a hysterical argument happens on the surface, but a character who is free-thinking in a *1984*-style world, where thinking freely is highly hazardous to one's personal safety, has conflict beneath the surface. Even when Winston Smith is not trying to avoid Big Brother, there is an implied conflict between his life and the rest of that world.

It is highly desirable to have both types of conflict present and accounted for. Is there conflict that is acted out on the page? Is the protagonist somehow pitted against the world they inhabit, whether it's a government, an office, or an entire society? Is there conflict between characters, which is expressed through actions and words, as well as hidden desires and thoughts that go unspoken? Does the character have competing interior desires and thus live in conflict with themselves? (The correct answer to all these questions is "yes.")

It can sometimes feel a little icky to always be hitting the conflict button, but unless you are intentionally and specifically choosing to have a quiet moment, you should always look for ways to introduce some degree of conflict.

Why? Because a character totally at peace with their surroundings and the people they're interacting with is completely boring. Sure, give them a quiet moment from time to time, but this moment should be a respite from conflict, or should set up a future conflict, rather than being a gaping void of conflict.

The best way to introduce conflict is to place obstacles in the way of your characters. Conflict happens when a character tries to surmount an obstacle (for instance, a character negotiating with a cop who has stopped and delayed them or an alcoholic trying to say no to a drink) or when two characters have conflicting motivations that create an obstacle (one character wants to break up and the other wants to stay together). Conflict is all about how characters try to overcome obstacles in order to get what they want.

Conflict also impacts the flow of a novel. Much like music, novels have a rhythm. Once you hit the middle stretch of writing a novel, it can sometimes become difficult to keep the beat.

Whether they realize it or not, readers expect things to unfold at a certain speed. In the beginning of a novel, things can unfold slowly or quickly, but a basic rhythm is established at the outset. The reader internalizes this and sets their expectations based on how things unfold in the first fifty pages, with the expectation that the speed will gradually ramp up as you head for the end.

If you're ever thinking to yourself, "Man, this is getting slow" or "Where is all *this* stuff coming from?" it probably means the author has lost the pace they had previously established.

Pacing is marked by the length of time between moments of conflict.

When a conflict arises in a novel, the reader wants to find out how it is resolved. When a character commits a crime, the reader wants to find out if the character is going to get caught. When one character has a fight with another character, the reader wants to know if they're going to make up. The more conflict you introduce and the quicker things happen, the faster the pace.

If there is a very slow stretch in a novel, it's often because there's no conflict: things are just happening, the author is indulging in exposition that's not woven into the plot, or events are transpiring that are unrelated to the big unanswered question that had been driving the action. When this happens, the reader isn't sure why they should care.

If there are places where things feel like they're starting to wander, think about how you can introduce conflict or tie things back to the main plot arcs. Or, if you're too relentless with the action and you're worried you're exhausting the reader, find a way to have a quieter scene that fills an important role in the narrative but doesn't represent all-out conflict.

Ultimately, conflict is the reason we read novels. It forces characters to make decisions. It tests their strengths and weaknesses. It reveals how they think, how they react to pressure, and what makes them tick. Readers want to see whether the conflicts will be resolved and how the conflicts will be resolved, and they want to see who gets what they want, who wins, and how they win.

Remember, a man contentedly walking down the street is not a story. It only becomes a story when he is captured by space monkeys that force him to slap himself in the face over and over and say "I'm hitting myself."

Now that is conflict.

Rule #21
CREATE ROMANCE AND RIVALRY

John Green's *Looking for Alaska* is a (deservedly) much-loved and much-awarded young adult novel; if you haven't read it, you might consider dropping this guide to writing a novel and going to read it. You can come back here when you're done.

(Don't worry, I'll wait.)

For those who have *Looking for Alaska* on their perennial "gap" book list and who would like me to just get on with the chapter, the basic plot is this: a boy, quickly nicknamed "Pudge" by his roommate, "The Colonel," is attending a boarding school. Pudge develops a very strong crush on a girl named Alaska (not a nickname), who is beautiful but flighty, uneven, and intense. She has a boyfriend, but she seems somewhat intrigued by Pudge, and their relationship forms the backbone of the book as they embark upon pranks and hijinks in an attempt to survive life at school.

While John Green possesses many things you can't teach, like a pitch-perfect ear and what must be a painfully photographic memory of precisely what it's like to be in high school, the way Green crafts the relationship between Pudge and Alaska is an incredible illustration of how to develop an interesting relationship between two characters.

Every single interaction between Pudge and Alaska advances their relationship, moving it forward in a series of incremental steps that swing between positive and negative emotion, with each interaction growing more intense.

One encounter leaves Pudge feeling like Alaska is the greatest girl in the world, but a minute later he feels as if she's ignoring him or being mean to him. In the next encounter, he feels as if she's the most fantastic creature in the entire universe, but in the encounter after that, he feels as if he may pass out from how much she despises him. Every time he experiences a swing between positive and negative, he feels it more acutely than the previous time because he is steadily becoming more invested in the relationship.

If you were to map out the highs and lows of their interactions over the course of the book, it would look like a mountain range where every peak is taller and steeper than the last.

Some of these swings are due to Alaska's wild personality, but this is an almost textbook way to develop an intense relationship on the page. The variance between up and down moments creates suspense as the reader wonders which way the relationship will end up going, and the reader becomes increasingly invested in the relationship as well. Each time the line swings up to a positive experience, it feels earned because Pudge had to suffer through the last negative one.

This same essential dynamic can also be used to build rivalries between two characters, where an initial negative encounter can steadily escalate over time into outright hatred. A bully can start simply by punching a character in the shoulder, but that character can escalate things by gluing the bully's locker closed, while the bully can retaliate by stuffing the character in a trash can, and pretty soon they're on their way to all-out war.

Too often when new writers try to craft jousting or intense relationships between characters, the relationships feel one-note because the characters have roughly the same mixed, sparring interactions over the course of the book, perhaps with a positive spike if they get together/make peace or a negative spike if they split/remain enemies.

When every interaction ends in the same mixed place, there isn't the same feeling of investment and suspense in the conflict. If the relationship doesn't grow in intensity or change dynamics, or if there's no mystery in how the two characters will feel about each other or who will gain the upper hand in the end, the reader will quickly decide they know what they need to know about the relationship and won't be particularly interested in what happens.

On the other hand, when the relationship-o-meter swings between positive and negative poles, it somehow feels more true to life. It feels like things could end up anywhere. When you add increasing intensity to the ups and downs, the reader won't be able to turn the page fast enough to find out what happens.

What's most interesting to me about this dynamic is that it's not generally how real life works. Our opinions about people do not tend to swing wildly back and forth based on every interaction we have with them. For the most part, our encounters with the people we care about don't end on definitively positive or definitively negative moments and cut to a chapter break. Even when we fight, things tend to feel somewhat mixed and muddled.

On the page, though, it works beautifully. The quick swings between up and down in *Looking for Alaska* evoke the confusion and intensity of first love. We feel more connected to the relationship because the characters have to earn it. We learn more about Pudge and Alaska by seeing how they deal with and adapt to different magnitudes of feelings. In other novels, steady escalations between two enemies ratchet up the tension and keep us glued to see who will win.

Make sure your characters have dynamic relationships that swing between the positive and the negative. Whenever two characters feel intensely about each other, this formula helps bring the relationship to life.

Rule #22
DON'T LET A CHARACTER "LOSE" THE READER

We touched previously on how characters in first person narratives have to be compelling enough to pass the elevator test, but there is another line between sympathetic and unsympathetic characters that's important to bear in mind.

Let's start with a question: Why do we like some characters who do horrible things and dislike the heck out of some goody two-shoes?

Basically, it all comes down to the concept of "redeemability."

Redeemability involves more than just actions. We've seen lots and lots of characters in novels and movies who do utterly horrible things, and yet we still find them compelling enough to read on (Humbert Humbert from *Lolita* is Exhibit A, B, and C of this phenomenon).

But if characters are going to consistently do bad things and retain the reader's sympathy, they have to be compelling. They have to be brave or brilliant or hilarious or charismatic or strong or all the above. They have to possess some qualities that we admire in such ample quantities that it manages to balance out the bad. We wouldn't normally like someone who eats human flesh, but isn't Hannibal Lecter smart and kind of hilarious?

They have to have charisma.

Word math: charisma – bad actions = redeemability

Now, redeemability is a fickle beast. If a character's redeemability meter dips below a certain base line, the character will "lose" the reader. We've all experienced such moments, when an uncharismatic character did something so horrible and shocking and irredeemable that there was no going back, like when Dolores Umbridge punished Harry Potter in that horrible, horrible way, where he had to write "I must not tell lies" with that blood quill and . . . I am cringing so much writing this, I can't even type the rest of what happened.

The redeemability meter often dips below zero when a character does something that's wrong, or disproportionately harsh relative to the situation, and there's not sufficient explanation for their actions. They weren't misguided or deluded or well-intentioned-but-astray. They didn't have an excuse. They just went and did it, and the reader concludes: they're just evil.

There's no going back. The reader will make some (but not endless) allowances for a really compelling character who acts badly, but unlikability combined with unmotivated evil actions will result in a character "losing" the reader. The worse the action, the more insanely likable a character has to be.

Proportion is just as important. If someone has a good reason to be angry but then goes and slaughters an entire village, this may be beyond the pale. There are also characters whose charisma levels are so low that it doesn't matter what good deeds they do, as the reader won't like them.

It's fine for a villain to lose the reader. In fact, you may employ this strategy to great effect to reinforce the stakes in the novel, just as J.K. Rowling did with Dolores Umbridge. It's also fine for a hero to lose the reader if you're going all Greek tragedy on us and the hero is suffering for their fatal flaw in the climax.

But a protagonist, particularly a narrator, just can't lose the reader before the absolute end of the book, and maybe not even then. It's crucial that the protagonist, the person with whom the reader most identifies, has the reader's attention and sympathy throughout the novel. If this character loses the reader, the reader will stop caring.

And then they'll stop reading.

Rule #23
LET THEM SEE YOUR CHARACTERS SWEAT

George R.R. Martin's novel *A Game of Thrones*, and the *Song of Ice and Fire* series as a whole, is known for many things, including for serving as the basis of an HBO series and for being the gold standard for gritty modern fantasy. But above all, as a "Better Book Title" blog parody indicated, *A Game of Thrones* may as well be titled "Don't Get Too Attached."

When people warn you not to get too attached to Martin's characters, they are usually referring to how the people who die in Martin's novels aren't the people you expect to die. He shows a remarkable capacity for killing off characters. Anyone can die at any moment, and Martin uses this unpredictable atmosphere to terrific effect.

However, I'd argue that Martin's lack of sentimentality goes even further, and there's a lesson here for all writers: Martin lets his characters have flaws.

Every character in *A Game of Thrones* has a set of positive and negative qualities and shows a full range of humanity. And Martin is not afraid to go dark. Even Ned Stark, arguably the noblest character in the book, has a somewhat inglorious past. He suffers from hubris. He can be sanctimonious. He is said to have fathered an illegitimate child. He is on the whole a good person, but he's flawed.

We writers can get really, really attached to our characters. They become almost like family members. We want the best for them. And sometimes it becomes difficult to see them make mistakes, to see their flaws, and to let the bad qualities shine through from time to time.

We can be way too nice to them.

This goes further, too; sometimes we don't think enough about how to test characters through their weaknesses. When you're placing obstacles in your character's way, don't just think about how they can overcome these obstacles with their best qualities, but think about which situations will challenge them and how their bad qualities could lead to their possible defeat or downfall.

Let your characters fail sometimes. Let the reader see their bad side, their cranky side, or their hubristic side.

Better yet, construct the entire novel around the idea that you need to find a way to show the entire spectrum of your character. Sometimes they rise to the occasion and sometimes they are brought down a notch or three by their flaws. We should see the entire range over the course of a novel.

Showing a few warts won't make your readers dislike your characters. If anything, the characters will seem more human. Martin, for one, has no compunctions about showing his characters' warts, or even reveling in them, as he trusts that the readers will still feel affection for the characters.

As you weave these character choices into your plot, in the back of your head you may have the idea that you somehow have to choose between writing a plot-oriented novel and a character-oriented novel, and that one has to come at the expense of the other, but don't worry about these categories. It's a completely false choice.

Writers love to divide themselves into warring camps of competing ideals, and you can hear the tremendous outpouring of snootiness when this happens.

"Oh, I write *character-based* novels. I like my readers to actually get to know a real character instead of stuff just blowing up."

"Oh, I write genre fiction, and I do so proudly. Stuff actually, ya know, *happens* in my books."

See what these fictional people did? They separated themselves into "character" writers and "plot" writers. *Annnnnd* they're both wrong. Plot and character are inseparable.

Here's why.

Let's first look at what makes a compelling character. Here are some examples:

- A character starts off seeming normal, but the events that follow reveal abilities and/or personality traits they never knew they had (Luke Skywalker, Harry Potter, Anastasia Steele, et al.).
- A character battles internal demons, which places them at odds with their surroundings (Holden Caulfield, Hamlet, Quentin Compson, Anastasia Steele, et al.).
- A relatively normal person observes a crazy world around them (Ishmael, Nick Carraway, Arthur Dent, Anastasia Steele, et al.).

There are many more, and sometimes these different character archetypes are mixed up and combined. But what do they have in common? Stuff happens to them. They do stuff. Things get complicated. And, as we learned in Rule #20, at the heart of every compelling character who has walked the pages of a novel is one thing: conflict.

Or rather, three things: conflict, more conflict, and still more conflict.

How is that most-interesting character's personality revealed? Through the plot! What good is an interesting character if they aren't doing anything and if interesting things aren't happening to them? Character is what makes the plot interesting, because we're learning more about the character based on how they react to the events. The plot tests a character and forces them to make choices, and the plot needs a compelling character for us to care about it.

If the character isn't a different person at the end of the story than the beginning, well, that's not very interesting.

Plot needs character. Character needs plot. They're two sides of the same coin. Focus on developing them both in tandem, and don't neglect one at the expense of the other.

And don't be afraid to use the plot to uglify those characters.

Rule #24

BE UNPREDICTABLE

Storytelling is all about reversals, and we humans are drawn to them like crazy people to the *Bachelor* house. We love to see humble people get big, the big get knocked down, and the knocked down recover.

Reversals are moments where the direction of a narrative reverses: the weak grow strong or the strong grow weak.

Tatooine farmboys forego power convertors at the Tosche Station to become intergalactic heroes. Greek kings accidentally marry their mothers and fall from grace. Or something subtle can happen, like a character quietly gaining the upper hand in a conversation and setting a relationship on a new course.

These reversals of fortune are at the heart of good storytelling. Characters find success, they crash and burn, they find redemption, they crash and burn again, and maybe they get back on top again. Even during a good conversation, you'll find jousting reversals as two characters try to best one another and get what they want.

Similar to what I outlined in the earlier chapter on dynamic character relationships, a character's plot arc should follow a path of ups and downs. A good reversal, up or down, can jar your reader and grip them with drama.

I'm going to use *Star Wars* as an example, even though it isn't a novel, because chances are you've seen it, and this stuff applies to all stories, no matter the medium. And also because of Jawas.

So! In *Star Wars*, Monsieur Skywalker goes through a series of reversals:

- Bored, unable to go to Tosche Station to pick up power converters (down)
- A droid with a lot of carbon-scoring has a holographic message! Cool! (up)
- Assaulted by sand people (down)
- Rescued by Obi-Wan Kenobi! Takes possession of lightsaber! (up)
- Aunt and uncle are gruesomely killed by stormtroopers posing as sand people, traumatizing a generation (very down)
- Finds Han Solo and blasts off! Smell ya later, Greedo! (up)

- Trapped on Death Star; Alderaan destroyed by jerkish Grand Moff Tarkin (down)
- Finds the princess! (up)
- Nearly drowned by disgusting trash-snake-eyeball thing; about to be smashed by slowly moving compactor (down)
- Rescued by droids! (up)
- Obi Wan dead? Nooooo! (down)
- Fights off TIE Fighters (up, don't get cocky)
- Han Solo refuses to go on the mission to destroy the Death Star (down)
- Luke charges ahead anyway! Red 5 on the way! (up)
- Darth Vader has Luke in his sights (down)
- Han Solo has a change of heart! Take that, Vader! (up)
- Death star: KABOOM! Awkward medal ceremony! (very up, except for Chewbacca, who was screwed out of a medal)

So you see, Luke has a pretty consistent series of up and down reversals throughout the narrative.

He also has one major reversal over the course of the entire story, which is the huge transformation from a quiet farm boy to an intergalactic hero.

Even when you look at the trilogy as a whole, you see reversals:

- End of *Star Wars*: Destroys Death Star; receives medal (up)

- End of *The Empire Strikes Back*: Hand forcibly removed by Darth Vader/father; Han Solo trapped in carbonite (down)
- End of *The Return of the Jedi*: New Death Star blown up; Emperor defeated; Vader redeemed (up)

Reversals, reversals, reversals!

On the scene-to-scene level, on the beginning-to-the-end-of-a-novel/movie level, and on the series level.

Plot out your reversals and tie them to the tentpoles described in Rule #17. The major events in your novel should roughly follow an up/down/up pattern. Sometimes you might follow a major down moment with another one that's even worse in order to surprise the reader or to heighten the intensity of a character's despair, but there should be some alternation.

For instance, here are the tentpoles in *Jacob Wonderbar and the Cosmic Space Kapow*:

- The kids blast off into space and break the universe (up: they may have destroyed several uninhabited planets, but who cares, they're in space)
- Mick Cracken maroons Jacob and Dexter on a planet that smells like burp breath (down: tensions mount)
- Jacob and Dexter argue, and Jacob is captured by wacky scientists (very down: things beginning to seem hopeless)

- Sarah and Dexter are reunited, and they help save Jacob from a band of angry substitute teachers (up: together again!)
- Jacob ultimately decides to postpone his search for his possibly lost-in-space father, and the children go home (very up: everything is okay again)

If you make sure you're alternating between up and down and increasing the intensity, you'll keep the reader gripping the story.

BE MYSTERIOUS

One of the most important skills every writer has to master, no matter their genre, is how to craft a mystery in a novel. It's also one of the most misunderstood elements of novel writing.

Mysteries are the lures that keep us turning the pages and keep us glued to the book because we're dying to know what happens. Is the detective going to find the murderer? Is the couple going to get together? What happened on that fateful night? Will the protagonist's hatred of saxophones be his undoing?

The best stories also have smaller secondary and tertiary mysteries that keep the readers turning the pages.

When it comes to crafting a mystery, I sometimes think that newish authors get distracted by the bodies and the murders and the stereotypical elements, and they miss what really drives a great mystery. Good mysteries are not created simply by withholding information from the reader.

Mysteries are about people. And, in what might seem like a familiar refrain, every mystery starts with a character who wants something.

The character wants the woman to fall in love with him or he wants to catch the killer or he wants to find the truth about what happened or he wants to escape with his life. We keep reading to find out if the characters are going to get it. This is the heart of every mystery: Is the character going to get what they want? The greater the character's desire to get what they want, the greater the stakes and the consequences of getting it or not getting it; the greater the obstacles and intrigue and the longer things linger . . . the greater the mystery. Basically, we're reading to find out if something a character wants is going to happen.

Let's break that down into word math:

character's desire and the consequences/stakes + obstacles/intrigue + delay = mystery

Here's what that means:

DESIRES AND CONSEQUENCES

The first step in crafting a mystery is showing what your character wants and what the stakes are. If you show your character caring about something, it plants the appropriate question in the reader's mind (are they going to get what they want?) along with a sense of the consequences (dear God, what will happen to them if they don't get what they want?).

Is the cop going to find the murderer? Is the girl going to get the guy? Is the depressed penguin going to find its purpose?

The reason we care about the outcome of these questions is because there is an important character who cares deeply about the outcome. The more they care, the more *we* care about what happens and the more nervous we will be on their behalf if it looks like the outcome is in doubt.

And, of course, characters want to stay alive above all, so mysteries that have great danger are some of the best because they have the most significant stakes.

OBSTACLES AND INTRIGUE

The next step is placing roadblocks in front of your characters that prevent them from immediately getting the thing they want. What good is a mystery if it's easy to solve? What good is it to wonder about whether a girl is going to get a guy if he says yes immediately?

If you want your reader's spine to tingle with fear, you may also introduce some intrigue in the form of tantalizing hints, creepy details, and an atmosphere of danger or uncertainty. If you want them to feel titillated about a possible romance, you can introduce some misunderstandings, false starts, and alluring distractions.

The more difficult and insurmountable the mystery seems, the more your reader will be curious about the ultimate answer.

DELAY

This is the part where some writers go astray. A great mystery is built by prolonging the suspense. The longer we have to wait to find out who the killer is or find out whether two characters will get together, the greater our anticipation of that reward.

But sometimes writers try to create this delay by simply holding out on the reader and failing to share information that the characters would otherwise have known. This is the writing equivalent of playing keep-away with your reader while yelling "Neener neener neener" at them.

If a character knows exactly what happened and the author is simply withholding the information from the reader, it starts to feel like a contrived way of creating a delay. When failing to reveal the answer to the mystery doesn't make narrative sense, the reader will know that the author is just holding out on them.

Instead, good mysteries feature a character trying to get what they want, and we know what they know, but the truth is obscured or confusing or surprising or not what was anticipated. The object of desire lies just beyond their grasp, and it takes them a while to solve it. They might know that they're in danger, but they don't know what's going on either, and we are just as unsure as they are about whether they're going to get out alive or not.

As a character tries to figure out how to get what they want, the delay before they get there is what prolongs and deepens the mystery. They should have to work hard in order to solve it.

The better you are able to articulate your characters' fears and desires, the greater the mystery the reader will experience. If the stakes are high, the reader won't be able to turn the pages fast enough to find out what happens.

Rule #26
CREATE A GREAT SETTING

One of the best things about reading novels is the way they open up new worlds to us, whether it's a mystical kingdom, the far reaches of outer space, a period in ancient history, the distant future, somewhere in the real world that we've never visited, or a place that we've not seen in quite the same way before. It's an incredible experience to be immersed in an unfamiliar setting where vivid scenes and backdrops are brought to life.

But the best worlds are made of more than just the trees that dot the hillsides or the stars in outer space. There's a whole lot more to creating a great setting than simply figuring out the look and feel of the place where the novel is set.

Instead, the best settings feel like living, breathing places of their own. They are not paintings. They are three-dimensional spaces that have their own order, logic, and life.

There are four essential elements to a good setting:

CHANGE IS UNDERWAY

The best settings are not static, unchanging places that have no impact on characters' lives. Instead, in the best worlds, there is a plot inherent to the setting itself.

It could be a place in turmoil (*The Lord of the Rings*), a place that is resisting change but where there are tensions roiling the calm (*To Kill a Mockingbird*), or a place where an old era is passing in favor of a new generation (*The Sound and the Fury*).

Basically, something important is happening in the broader world that affects the characters' lives. There are forces outside of their control, and the things that are changing in the world interfere with the characters' lives (or the characters themselves may have a huge impact on these events).

Great settings are dynamic. Change is happening, and we have the sense that things will never be the same again.

PERSONALITY AND VALUES

There is more to a great setting than just the change that is underway, however.

A great setting has its own value system. Certain traits are ascendant and prized, whether it's valor and honor (*The Lord of the Rings*), justice and order (*Hondo*), or every man for himself (*The Road*). It could also be a place where normal values and perspectives have become skewed or inverted due to outside forces (*Catch-22*).

There's a personality and an outlook to these settings that throws us off kilter and makes us imagine how we'd react if we were placed in the same circumstances as the characters. They make us wonder if we would have the personal constitution to thrive within such places.

And, best of all, seeing places with unique values makes us look at our own surroundings in a brand new way.

Know and understand the values of your world. Who is a hero in this world? Who is a villain? Who are the celebrities? What are the religions? What is the government, who is in charge, and how are the laws decided?

Once you know the values, you can place your characters in line with these values or in opposition to them.

UNFAMILIARITY

Most importantly, a great setting shows us something we've never seen before. Either it's a place that most readers are unfamiliar with and have never traveled to (*The Kite Runner*), or it's a place that we are all too familiar with but is shown with a new, fresh perspective that makes us look at it again (*And Then We Came to the End*).

Whether it's a bar in Tennessee or a family's living room on another planet, you, as the author, have to take us someplace that has a sense of uniqueness and specificity. You have the ability to take us behind doors that are normally locked to us or that are unreachable because of time or distance. You can give us a glimpse of life that we can only receive through your novel.

Know this above all: What is in the world of your novel that your reader hasn't seen before? Even if it's meant to be a familiar setting, how does the setting show everyday places in a new way?

ILLUSTRATIVE DETAIL

Great authors are able to immerse the reader in their novels by describing the precise way the blades of grass on the hillsides wave in the wind, the pungent smell of ale in the taverns, and the sound of the crowds in the coliseums.

Whether the details are intended to draw a marked contrast between our planet and an alien land or point out the quirks we may not always notice in our coffee shops or workplaces, the details create a sense of place and force the reader to imagine themselves in that location.

When all these elements mesh together, and when the characters become swept up in the broader changes sweeping through a uniquely described setting, it elevates the plot by giving it a deeper and larger canvas upon which to paint the story.

Even if the characters aren't saving the world or confronting the changes head-on, the best plots intersect with their settings just as the events in the broader canvas exert themselves on the characters. This ultimately gives us a sense of the characters in a very unique time and place; they are partially able to control their surroundings, but they are also subject to forces outside their control.

When you think of where your characters are living, don't think of the place as a pretty backdrop behind them, but rather think of it as something that lives and breathes on its own. Think about your world as a character unto itself. It will never be the same after the novel ends.

Rule #27
FIND YOUR VOICE

Now that you have your plot, characters, and setting, it's time to start refining your writing, especially your voice. The problem is, voice is one of the most difficult aspects of writing to define and pinpoint.

You will often hear in your writing life that agents, editors, and readers want a "new voice" and a "compelling voice" and voice voice voice. We might know it when we see it, but what is voice, really? How do you cultivate it? How do you know when you have it? How many rhetorical questions do you think I can fit into this chapter?

Voice, at the most basic level, is the *sensibility* with which an author writes. It's a perspective, an outlook on the world, and a personality and style that is recognizable even out of context. If you were randomly dropped into a David Sedaris story or an Ernest Hemingway novel, you could probably guess the author within a few paragraphs because they have strong, unique voices. A great author's voice is often imitated, but a truly original voice can never be duplicated.

Here are the essential elements that comprise a novel's voice:

DISTINCT STYLE

At its heart, voice is about style.

Not just style in the sense of punctuation and how the prose looks on the page (though that can play a role), but style in the sense of a flow, a rhythm, a cadence to the writing, along with the vocabulary, lexicon, and slang that are used.

A voice can be wordy (William Faulkner), or it can be spare (Ernest Hemingway). It can be stylish and magical (Jeanette Winterson), or it can be wry and gritty (Elmore Leonard). It can be tied to unique times and places (Toni Morrison), or it can be almost wholly invented (Anthony Burgess).

Regardless of what is happening on the page, the prose should have a unique flavor.

A PARTICULAR PERSONALITY

A good voice has a personality of its own.

There's an *outlook* that is expressed in a voice.

It's a unique way of seeing the world and choosing which details to focus on and highlight. This doesn't necessarily mean that it's the author's personality coming through, just that the book itself has a style that conveys a unique view.

Think of how *Catch-22* captured the absurdity of World War II by boiling down irrational rules and presenting them at face value, or think of how *A Clockwork Orange* re-imagines the world through an intensely violent prism. Roald Dahl conveys a slightly sinister tone by breezily describing harrowing events, such as James' parents getting run over by a rhinoceros in *James and the Giant Peach*, while J.K. Rowling conveys a cheerfully magical tone using key details, such as the personalities of the moving paintings in *Harry Potter and the Sorcerer's Stone*.

These books convey tone through the descriptions and the style of narration, which creates a unique, unmistakable feeling for the reader.

CONSISTENCY

A good voice is consistent throughout a novel. It may get darker or lighter or funnier or sadder, but it doesn't suddenly shift wildly from whimsical to RAGEFUL (unless, of course, the voice is capable of making that stretch and the intent is to show such a drastic change).

The voice shouldn't be lost when the plot shifts. It shouldn't start sounding one way and finish sounding another. If you find your voice, or settle into it, later in the novel, it's important to go back and make it consistent throughout.

MODERATION

Even the strongest voices avoid overdoing it. Voices are not simply made up of repeated verbal tics ("You know," "like," "so I mean," "I was all," etc.), as they are much more nuanced than this. Nor are they transcriptions of real-life dialogue, as they only give the *impression* of a real-life voice and remain a unique construct. (More on dialogue in Rule #28.)

A voice shouldn't overwhelm the reader. If a writer focuses on voice to the exclusion of good plotting and characterization, it will feel like a shallow reading experience. Voice can help transport the reader to a new place, but the events of the novel and the compelling characters will be what carry the day.

IMMERSIVENESS

A good voice envelops the reader within the world of the book. It puts us in a certain frame of mind and lets us see the world from someone else's perspective. It provides not only the details of the world, but also a sense of the characters in that world, so that we truly feel that we are somewhere else.

This can be accomplished by employing regional slang and dialect (though they should be used in moderation) or by giving the prose style a certain edge, such as a spry, hard edge (Elmore Leonard's *Out of Sight*) or a soft, magical focus (Jeanette Winterson's *The Passion*). In these novels, the style of the voice embodies the setting of the novel.

AUTHORITY

A voice has to be strong enough that a reader gives themselves wholly to the author and becomes lost in the book. This means that the reader trusts the abilities of the author, and they aren't distracted by the writer's technique.

A good voice is confident and unwavering. You never see the author's hand in the books, as the voice is so convincing that the reader gives themselves over completely.

ORIGINALITY

Above all, a good voice is unique and can't be duplicated. Don't sweat it if the originality of your voice doesn't come right away, as you may have to keep writing to find it, but it should be there when everything is finished.

Your voice is in you. It's not *you* per se, but it's made up of bits and pieces of you. It may be how your sense of humor is expressed, or perhaps your whimsy or your cynicism, or your frustrations, hopes, or honesty, all of it distilled down (or dialed up) into a voice.

We leave fingerprints all over our work. These pieces of you in your work are what makes your writing something that can't be duplicated.

There is only one way to find this great voice: keep writing.

TALK THE TALK

Now that you've found your voice, here's how you can find your *characters*' voices through their dialogue.

The most important thing to remember is that dialogue in a novel has very little to do with how people actually talk in real life. Cultivating a sense of authenticity is important in novels, but that doesn't mean you should try to precisely capture the way people speak.

Do not try to write dialogue as people actually converse in real life, and don't ever defend yourself from criticism by saying, "But this is how people really talk." Set real life aside when it comes to dialogue in a novel, because the types of conversations that work in novels are rather unique.

If you don't imitate real-life speech, what do you do instead? Here are some tips:

GOOD DIALOGUE IS NOT WEIGHED DOWN BY EXPOSITION

When the dialogue is full of exposition and tries to tell the reader too much, the characters end up saying a lot of very unnatural and unwieldy things. You'll see things like:

"Remember that time we stole the frog from Miss Jenkins and she ended up giving us two hours of detention and that's how we met?"

"Yeah, totally! And now we're in sixth grade and have to dissect frogs for our science project, which is due tomorrow. I don't know how we're going to get it finished on time or why we're telling each other all of this since we both already know it!"

As the joke at the end indicates, virtually everything in this dialogue would have already been apparent to the characters. Without having to talk about it, they'd already know how they met, they'd already know they were in the sixth grade, and they'd already know the science project was due, and because of this, they wouldn't talk about it directly.

It's very clear what's really happening here: they're talking to the reader.

Exposition and dialogue only mesh when one character genuinely doesn't know what the other character is telling them and when it's logical within the plot for them to explain it at the precise moment they're explaining it.

Otherwise, if you're just trying to smush exposition into a conversation, your reader is going to spot it a mile away. It won't feel natural.

GOOD DIALOGUE HAS A PURPOSE AND BUILDS TOWARD SOMETHING

Sometimes you'll see characters bantering back and forth in a way that is meant to reveal character or fill space, but unless it's just so insanely and unbelievably clever that a writer somehow makes it work, this hollow banter will feel, uh, hollow.

A good conversation is an *escalation*. The dialogue is about something, and it builds toward something. If things stay even and neutral, the dialogue will feel empty or pointless.

Characters in a novel never just talk. There's always something more to it. It should be a conversation that you would want to eavesdrop on; when it's over, you should be nodding to yourself because you have a sense of where things ended.

GOOD DIALOGUE EVOKES THE WAY PEOPLE TALK IN REAL LIFE WITHOUT ACTUALLY BEING LIKE THE WAY PEOPLE TALK IN REAL LIFE

In real life, our conversations wander all over the place, and any conversation transcribed from real life will be a meandering mess full of free association and stuttering. In a novel, good conversations are focused, and they are, for the most part, articulate.

When we talk in real life, we pepper our words with interjections and ums and slang, but it would be hugely annoying and confusing on the page if every start and stop were faithfully written down. It would be even worse if we stuck faithfully to accents and regional dialects, which we're far more forgiving of when hearing them in person than when seeing them transcribed on the page, where they can feel exhausting.

Instead, think of dialect and slang like jalapeño peppers: a little bit can add some spice and flavor, but adding too much will make you spit out your food.

GOOD DIALOGUE REVEALS PERSONALITY, AND CHARACTERS ONLY RARELY SAY PRECISELY WHAT THEY ARE THINKING

Despite all the words at our disposal, words tend to fail us at key moments. Even when we know what we want to say, we spend a great deal of time and effort trying to articulate what we feel, while rarely being able to do it quite properly.

We misunderstand, overemphasize, underemphasize, and grasp at what we mean. Conversations go astray. So when two characters go back and forth, explaining exactly what they are feeling and thinking, it doesn't seem remotely real.

Good dialogue instead comprises *attempts* at articulation. There's a whole lot that is kept back. We only rarely put our true feelings out there.

This caginess shouldn't be taken too far, and a conversation shouldn't be an endless string of misunderstandings, unless you're Samuel Beckett. But how characters express their feelings is one of the most important ways to reveal character.

Are they reserved? Boisterous? Do they bluster? Hold back?

Characters who say exactly what they mean are generic. Characters who talk around their emotions and objectives are much more interesting.

GOOD DIALOGUE GOES EASY ON THE EXCLAMATIONS AND EXHORTATIONS

When a character overuses "Ugh" and "Blech" and "God," they can easily sound petulant.

When they overuse "What!" and "Wow!" and "Shut up!" they can exhaust the reader with their excitability.

When they overuse "Um" and "I mean" and "So I," they can drive the reader crazy with their hesitation.

Use these sparingly. If ever.

GOOD DIALOGUE IS BOOSTED BY DIALOGUE TAGS, GESTURES, AND ACTION, AS THESE HELP THE READER FOLLOW WHO IS SAYING WHAT

Poor maligned dialogue tags! (Dialogue tag examples: he said, she said, he asked, she asked.)

Out there in the Land of Writing Advice, it is often trendy for people to advocate stripping dialogue tags out of novels, so the person who is speaking is solely apparent through gestures and context.

This is overkill. Get behind me, dialogue tags, and I will defend you until the end!

As long as you stick mainly to "he/she said" and "he/she asked," your reader isn't going to notice the dialogue tags at all. They are as invisible as the word "the." Don't overdo them, and look for ways to add meaningful gestures and actions to conversations, but don't throw the baby out with the bathwater.

The key with gestures and actions is not to simply use them to break up the dialogue for the purpose of pacing, but to actually make them meaningful.

GOOD DIALOGUE IS UNEXPECTED

There's nothing worse than reading a stretch of dialogue where the characters say precisely what the reader thinks they're going to say or where they are stating the obvious.

The best dialogue counters our expectations and surprises us.

"Vladimir Putin!"

Rule #29
WEAVE EXPOSITION NATURALLY INTO THE STORY

This is the key to exposition: give the reader the right information at the right time.

Simple, right?

Yeah. Not so much.

At some point while writing a novel, especially if you are creating a world that is vastly different from our own, it will be important to explain some stuff. Maybe you need to let the reader in on why your protagonist's government is ruled by malevolent giant squids or how the bridge trolls became unionized.

Everyone knows that infodumps are often boring and stilted. When characters sit down and start explaining things to each other, it can quickly feel unnatural and fling the reader out of the novel. Exposition can make a story stop feeling like a story and start feeling like a history lesson. Instead of being immersed in the narrative, the readers start imagining an author somewhere who is throwing up her hands and saying, "Crap! Now I have to explain how unicorns were invented. Kill me now."

There is one very important key to exposition that will help smooth out the reading experience:

THE INFORMATION IS TIED TO SPECIFIC EVENTS THAT ARE HAPPENING IN THE PLOT AT THE TIME OF THE EXPLANATION

That's it. As long as the information being explained is tied to the events that are happening in the story at that time, and as long as it's crucially important for the characters, the reader, or both to learn this information, it won't feel like an infodump. It will feel natural to the reader because they need the exposition at this time.

James Dashner's *The Maze Runner* is a masterful example of providing incremental exposition. The novel begins with a character, Thomas, who quite literally has no idea who he is or what is happening.

He gradually learns that he's in the center of a vast, deadly maze, and survival is by no means assured.

But Thomas's circumstances aren't explained to him all at once. It's not as if a character sits down with Thomas on page five and says, "So . . . hey . . . we're in this vast maze and people die, and here are all the rules the author wants the reader to know." Instead, Thomas learns about the world gradually, bit by bit, and he learns this information when it's important for him to know it during each specific scene.

You don't have to explain every single mysterious thing about your world right away. Readers have a remarkable capacity to go with the flow and accept that they don't know everything at first. In fact, this lack of knowledge can help preserve a healthy sense of mystery.

Instead, readers only have to know the information that is needed to understand the events transpiring at that precise moment.

There are two main ways of integrating exposition into a novel. If the character already knows the information that the reader needs to know, they can simply tell the reader. Ernest Cline's *Ready Player One* is a great example of this. The main character, Wade, knows his world backward and forward, and in fact a huge part of the plot hinges on his exhaustive knowledge of the online world in which much of the action is set. But instead of explaining every piece of its history all at once, Wade simply explains the information the reader needs to know when it's important to know it. Since the exposition is crucial to providing context to the events in the plot, it feels natural to the reader.

Or, if the character doesn't know the backstory, it's best to turn the acquisition of the information into a scene unto itself. This is how J.K. Rowling uses the pensieve in the *Harry Potter* novels. Instead of having Dumbledore explain key events to Harry through conversation, they use the pensieve to literally see the events transpire. Another way to approach this is for a character to learn the crucial info by sneaking into a library where the bad guys are lurking or to steal an important map from the pirate's lair. The character isn't just having information explained to them, as the act of acquiring the information itself is woven into the story.

Novels are a snapshot in time. In great novels, it feels as if there is a vast history that precedes the start of Chapter One and as if all the characters have rich backstories that influence the novel. But this history does not have to be explained all at once.

Instead, the information should arrive just when we need it.

Rule #30

IT'S ALL ABOUT THE CLIMAX

Saddle up the bronco, batten the hatches, take cover, and grab some popcorn.

It's climax time.

Near the end of the novel, your characters will confront their biggest obstacles, all the simmering plots and subplots will come to a head, and oh, yes, it helps if the climax comprises your best, most dramatic, and most surprising scenes, when the moments have the biggest weight and the characters are experiencing their highest highs and their lowest lows in quick succession, and the events have your reader cheering or crying or laughing or (preferably) all of the above (hopefully in a good way), and there is also TRIUMPH.

It's kind of a big deal.

If there is one piece of advice in this entire guide that you remember and act upon, it should be this: start planning your climax as soon as possible.

Yes, yes, I can hear the improvisers out there howling in outrage, but even if you're not a planner or an outliner, it's crucially important to give the climactic moment some thought. The sooner you know roughly what is going to happen in your climax, the sooner you can begin laying the groundwork in the plot.

This is because no matter how well-written your climax is, the power it possesses is almost entirely determined by what you have built over the course of the novel. Whether you have an exciting climax or a total dud is determined by how successful you were at ratcheting up the stakes before the climax, whether you gave the reader reasons to care about what happens as the climax approaches, and how well you set your characters up to face their biggest challenges.

Even if you're an improviser, the success of your novel will hinge on how well you build toward the ending. You may have to go back through and revise the plot events so that they lead to this moment, but there's no escaping how intertwined the success of a climax is with how well the foundation has been laid throughout the course of the novel.

Here are the elements of a great climax:

THE PROTAGONIST[S] FACE[S] THEIR MOST DIF-FICULT OBSTACLE[S]

Classic genre novels have this one easy: the protagonist faces off with the bad guy once and for all. Both the protagonist and the villain bring everything they have, there's a big battle, and we get to see who wins.

Even if you're not writing a genre novel, it's still important for your characters to face their biggest challenges/fears/desires of all. There doesn't need to be a gunfight, but there does need to be a sense that your character is being tested like they've never been tested before.

ALL THE MAJOR CONFLICTS INTRODUCED IN THE NOVEL ARE RESOLVED

Essentially, the climax is the place where we find out whether the characters get what they want. All the obstacles they've overcome, and all the physical and mental miles they've traveled, were simply a prelude to set the stakes for the climax. Now we find out if the protagonist is going to get the guy/girl, if they're going to overcome their addiction, if they're going to resolve the angst they feel toward their parents, or if that depressed penguin really is going to find his sense of purpose (please tell me! I must know!).

Now, if you are setting up a multi-book storyline, or if you prefer a little unsettled complexity in your novels, you don't have to tie every storyline up in a neat and tidy bow. We can still be left to wonder about some dangling threads, but the reader should be left with the satisfying sense that the main storyline feels resolved. Darth Vader might have flown off into space, but Luke succeeded at what he set out to accomplish: he was able to use the Force and destroy the Death Star.

It's also okay to resolve some of your storylines before the climax. Maybe a fight between two of your characters gets resolved earlier in the novel, and then they join forces for the climax. Or perhaps a subplot is wrapped up to set up the finale.

The more arcs your climax resolves, the more powerful and momentous it will feel.

WE LEARN ABOUT THE CHARACTERS THROUGH THE CHOICES THEY MAKE

The climax is the place that tests the characters the most, and we find out the result of their biggest choices. It is the point when a character's conflicting motivations battle it out, and we can see what they hold most dear.

In the climax of *Jacob Wonderbar and the Cosmic Space Kapow*, Jacob has to choose between going home with his friends and staying out in space to find his dad. He loves his friends, and yet he misses his dad terribly. How does he choose between these two things? The choice he makes, and the reasons for making it, ultimately reveal the qualities he values the most and who he is as a person.

Don't just raise the stakes for your characters in the external world. Give them internal stakes as well. Once the characters make their final choices, your reader will feel as if they truly know who these characters are.

THE EVENTS THAT TRANSPIRE ARE THE MOST INTENSE OF ALL

It's not enough to just resolve the different character arcs and call it a day. The climax should show off the best of *everything*.

All the events that have been roiling your setting in the background should come to the fore, and we should see the setting come alive. The scenes themselves must be exciting and charged and feature some of your best ideas and your best writing.

The stakes of the climax don't necessarily have to be life or death, but this is when we find out whether the characters will get the big thing they wanted, and the answer will arrive in the most intense fashion you can possibly dream up. The expression of this intensity can be exciting if it's a fantasy novel, scary if it's horror, hot if it's romance, or all the above if you're writing a romantic zombie fantasy.

The approach you take should be appropriate to your story, but even if you're writing literary fiction, it's crucial that your climax represents the pinnacle of emotion in the story.

One way to dial up this intensity is for your protagonist to experience their highest highs and their lowest lows in rapid succession either during or right around your climax. Your character might lose the person they love just as they win their biggest battle, or they might win the person they love as they lose their biggest battle.

In order to set up these four crucial parts of the climax, you have to lay all the groundwork in advance. If you're a planner, the climax is usually one of the easiest of all the stretches of your novel to write because you have already laid the groundwork leading up to this final stretch. By the time you reach your climactic scenes, you will know what will happen backward and forward, and you can just focus on making the scenes as thrilling as possible.

Or, if you're an improviser, you may just have to get to your climax, write what happens, make it as exciting as possible, and then go back through the earlier sections and layer in the emotions and motivations in order to give your climax the biggest punch.

The biggest mistake to avoid as you write your climax is to rush through it. The end of your novel will feel tantalizingly close as you near the finish line, and it's tempting to speed your way through. You will be so ready to just get your novel done and over with and become one of those exalted people who have finished a novel.

Instead? Take your time. Savor the pinnacle of your novel, and put your characters through hell. And heaven. And hell again. And then an even better heaven, one they never saw coming.

You get the idea.

TROUBLESHOOTING AND STAYING SANE

Rule #31
KEEP CALM AND CARRY ON

Writing the first fifty pages of a novel is like the honeymoon phase after you've fallen head over heels in love.

Everything is amazing! You couldn't be happier! It's so easy! You want to spend all your time with your novel! Everything you've ever attempted pales in comparison to the wondrousness of this! Exclamation points!!

Then, at some point, your novel will do something that annoys the living crap out of you. The shine will start to wear off.

Maybe it becomes monotonous. Or maybe one of the characters openly rebels against your plans. Or maybe it demands too much of your time when you'd rather just watch some television in peace.

This is an exceedingly dangerous time in your writing life, where you will be tested in ways you can't possibly imagine. By the fifty-page point, you have invested a huge amount of time and energy in your novel. You may have gotten further into a novel than ever before, and yet at some point it will always be difficult to keep going. The rush that you felt when you first started and everything was easy will have faded.

Page fifty is where you will know if you have found true novel-writing love or if you chose an idea you merely like.

If it's love, you have to find a way to power through. You have to crawl to your computer or notebook and force yourself to keep going even if you'd rather be doing anything else. And you will.

Here are five things that can help:

CULTIVATE YOUR FEAR OF FAILURE

Despite what Yoda may have you believe, fear does not always lead to anger, hate, and suffering. Fear is one of the best motivators you have as a writer. Invest in the idea of your novel and fear how much you would hate to leave it unwritten. Lean into the notion that you'll be letting yourself down if you don't finish. Put pressure on yourself. Be afraid of the regret you'll feel for the rest of your life if you don't accomplish your dream.

Fear is a feeling that can keep you going. Fear your own disappointment.

SET DEADLINES WITH TEETH

Deadlines don't actually work that well for me personally (they tend to succeed only in stressing me out), but I know people who swear by them. The trick is to set a deadline that you feel like you can't escape. Create a deadline with a real penalty. If you secretly know that the deadline you're setting for yourself is a soft one, it's not going to have its hair-raising, stress-inducing maximum effect.

So you either have to learn to be scared of yourself and your own self-punishments or you need a partner in crime who can help you keep up with them. You can let someone else fine you for your transgressions or you can stick to your own personal punishment plan.

In tandem, develop a matching rewards program. Want to watch that episode of *Real Housewives* after slogging through ten pages? Go for it. Want to treat yourself to a glimpse of Twitter after finishing a chapter? It's your prerogative.

Carrot and stick, baby. Carrot and stick.

DAYDREAM A LITTLE

It's okay to imagine what will happen if your book blows up, you are on the cover of 50 magazines, you are the toast of the literati, and you become a gazil-lionaire. While you can't let these dreams become such ironclad expectations that not achieving them darkens your mood, you can give yourself the freedom to imagine these best-case scenarios. Wildly improbable dreams are a surprisingly effective motivational tool.

When you reach a point where you don't feel like you can write another word, just imagine being so famous that the entire world is waiting with bated breath for you to finish your next chapter. Then give these imaginary people what they want.

BEFRIEND WRITERS WHO HAVE FINISHED A NOVEL

Before I knew experienced writers, the idea of writing a novel felt so impossibly impossible that the people who wrote them almost seemed as if they were surrounded by a magical novel-writing aura. But when you get to know the people behind the books, there's not much to the secret of how they accomplished it: they sat in place for as long as it took to write a novel.

Get to know some of these people. Lean on them. They may give you a blank, pitying, horrified stare when you start fretting that you're never going to finish your first novel and they've written several hundred of them, but that blank stare will shame you back to the keyboard in no time.

If they can do it, so can you.

YOU'RE WRITING SOMETHING YOU LOVE, RIGHT?

You have to love your novel unconditionally if you're going to finish.

Rule #32
BE SERIOUS ABOUT YOUR SERIES

If you are planning to write a standalone novel, you're in luck! You can skip this chapter. I promise we won't talk about you behind your back.

If, however, you have even an inkling of a thought that you may at some point wish to turn your novel into a series, read on.

If you're an unpublished author with a big idea, should you set out to write a series from the outset?

My opinion: it depends.

The first question you want to ask yourself is whether you want to pursue traditional publication or self-publication. If you're self-publishing: go for it. Write a series if you want to. The only thing stopping you from writing a hundred book series is your ability to think of enough character names.

However, if you have even a remote feeling that you first want to pursue traditional publication, I would approach a series with a great deal of caution.

Yes, series are popular, even debut series, especially in genre fiction of all types, although these things go in phases. And, yes, people love to read series, and they love to write them, too. But here's the thing: getting a first novel published traditionally is really, really difficult. And getting a second novel published can be even more difficult.

Since it's so difficult, you really need to go for broke with your first novel. You shouldn't be saving your best ideas for the third, fifth, or seventh book in a series that might not come to fruition. When you're starting out, you should go all-in on that one novel, throwing in everything, *including* the kitchen sink, and making your debut as stellar as possible. This first book should stand alone, whether or not it's eventually expanded into a series.

Sure, as you're writing that standalone first novel, you can leave a few threads dangling to keep open the possibility of revisiting the characters and the world, but the novel should be completely self-contained and satisfying on its own. Don't worry that you won't have enough material left for sequels. You'll definitely think of new ideas later.

If your eventual agent wants to pitch your novel as the first book in a series, and if a publisher is interested in making it a series, this is awesome! You have yourself a series. But if they think it should stand alone, this will be fine, too, because your standalone novel can, much like the proverbial cheese, happily stand alone.

If the publishing gods have not smiled upon you and helped you find a taker for that first novel, but you still want to have your next novel traditionally published: start a completely new book. Do not become afflicted with *acute sequelitis*.

Acute sequelitis is characterized by an aversion to starting fresh with a completely new project, even after being unable to place the first book in a series with a publisher. Authors suffering from *acute sequelitis* will then write a sequel, then the third in a trilogy, and pretty soon they will have six or ten or a dozen interconnected books, the fourth of which might actually be publishable . . . if it didn't need the first three books to make sense.

Agents and publishers are not going to spring for the sequel to an unpublished novel. If you want to draw upon the same world and characters in a new novel that stands completely alone and doesn't depend on the other novel: fine, go for it!

But most times it's important to leave the old world and characters behind and start fresh. As much as you feel like you captured irreplaceable lightning in a bottle with your first world, you will likely find yourself creating a new world that you like even better.

Also, if you are planning to write a series, you should strongly consider creating a Series Bible, which is essentially a comprehensive guide to your own books. Which sounds crazy, but trust me, you will not be able to remember everything you write.

At some point, when you are writing the second or third or tenth novel in your series, it will be necessary to describe a character that played a hugely important or terrifically minor role in a previous book, and you will try your hardest to think about what the character looks like . . . and you may get it completely wrong. You won't remember what color eyes they have or how many wives they've married. You can't keep every important detail of a series in your head. It's not possible. That's why you need a Series Bible.

Series Bibles take many different forms. Sometimes writers are hired to write an entry in an already-existing series or a line of books with certain rules (such as in romance), and the Series Bible will provide the characters, world, plotlines, and rules to follow in advance.

If this doesn't already exist, you should absolutely create your own. This way, whenever you reintroduce a character, the Series Bible will remind you exactly what they look like. If you have different worlds/ planets/lands/classrooms/lairs, you won't have to go through your dusty old manuscripts to remember which one is which and whether that vampire bat had red eyes or yellow eyes.

The Series Bible is a lifesaver when your brain has reached and exceeded its capacity, which will probably happen somewhere around page five of your first novel.

Here's what to include:

CHARACTERS AND RELATIONSHIPS

What they look like (just copy and paste descriptions straight from the book), how many brothers and sisters they have, important events in their past, personality traits, unique schedules (e.g., piano lessons, summer vacations), hobbies, and secret powers. Include all characters in the Series Bible, both major and minor. You never know who's going to reappear.

Also, keep tabs on who is related to whom, who used to be in a relationship with whom, who used to be friends with whom, and how the social fabric of your setting is stitched together.

LOCATIONS

Worlds/planets/lands/classrooms/lairs/bars/ apartments—include what they look like, their history and backstory, and their landmarks and identifying details.

RULES OF LAW

Any important/unique laws, rules, restrictions, etc. When you review your Series Bible, you may suddenly realize that you created a plot hole by previously making it against the law to eat pita bread. Observe your setting's laws and keep them holy.

ALL IMPORTANT BACKSTORY/HISTORY THAT HAPPENS OFF THE PAGE

Make sure you know and keep track of the key events that influence your characters. You can even include backstory that didn't make it into the actual novel to help you keep track of things that might eventually influence the events on the page, such as a dark episode in your protagonist's past that happened before the novel begins but that still haunts them.

INVENTIONS/SPECIAL POWERS

This is especially important for science fiction and fantasy. In addition to associating magical powers with individual characters, I suggest that you separately keep track of all the existing secret powers and inventions you've introduced. When you invent something, even when it's just barely mentioned, it can have huge repercussions for the rest of the story because it affects what is possible in the world of the novel.

For instance, if you introduce a personal teleportation drive, whenever a character is in trouble and the character fails to teleport themselves out of danger, your reader will be like, "Duh, use the personal teleportation drive. Dang it! USE THE PERSONAL TELEPORTATION DRIVE!!"

Keep track of all inventions and powers, make sure their rules of use are clearly delineated, and make sure they're consistent with each other.

ANYTHING ELSE YOU MAY NEED TO REMEMBER LATER

It's better to include something if it feels important than to forget about it until you've fallen deep into a plot hole and can't climb out.

Rule #33
GET BACK ON THE HORSE

At some point over the course of writing a novel, life will interfere. Those pesky people who like to call themselves "kids" and "relatives" and "spouses" will grow tired of your hermit routine and insist that you rejoin the world for things like births and weddings and other such nonsense.

Eventually, inevitably, your oh-so-productive writing routine will get interrupted. This can be a very dangerous time. Momentum, once lost, is difficult to regain. It's just like exercise. If you haven't worked out for a few weeks, the first time back is going to be painful.

I've known writers who hit their stride initially, but were then interrupted for one reason or another, and days turned into weeks, weeks turned into months, and they were never able to get back in the saddle. All their work was squandered:

Breaks = kryptonite-laced, termite-ridden, ankle-breaking, weakening destabilizers

Don't let long breaks destroy you!

Once your writing rhythm has been broken, here's how to get it back:

DON'T BE UPSET WITH YOURSELF FOR TAKING THE BREAK

Real life has to come before your novel, and sometimes events pop up and demand your immediate and/or sustained attention. Do not feel guilty. You were doing the right thing as a human being. Your novel may temporarily suffer, but that's okay. It will be worth it in the long run, and you will be able to get back on track.

Just do everything you can to ensure it's only a momentary setback.

DON'T HEAD STRAIGHT FOR THE NOVEL

On your first day back, instead of going right back to your novel and the crushing weight of the blinking cursor, begin by writing something, anything, other than fiction.

E-mails, blog posts, forum posts, unhinged letters to the editor of the local newspaper, you name it.

Chances are your time off has left you looking desultorily at all the things that have piled up and yet still need a response, and it's much easier to dash off an e-mail than to figure out what is going to happen next in your novel.

Don't procrastinate endlessly, but if you can get the words flowing, it makes for a much easier reentry when you're ready to get going with the novel again.

Then it's time to . . .

BADGER YOURSELF INTO OPENING YOUR NOVEL AND GETTING STARTED AGAIN EVEN IF IT FEELS LIKE YOU ARE PEELING OFF YOUR OWN SKIN

It can feel so incredibly intimidating to start writing your novel again. You might not remember where you left off. You might have gotten used to filling your time with old episodes of *Downton Abbey*.

Writing is hard. Getting back into writing is really, really hard.

Do whatever you have to do to get that file open. Curses and threats of bodily harm against yourself are perfectly acceptable. So are rewards and bribes. Just get the dang file or notepad open.

You need to get some words on the page.

START SOMEWHERE EASY

When you do crack open the old novel, start somewhere that will help you get things flowing and will keep your confidence high. Do you have a scene in mind that you want to write and you know how it will turn out, but you haven't arrived there chronologically in the plot? Jump ahead and write it anyway.

Need to do some revising to get back into the rhythm? Awesome, start there.

Are your chapter numbers out of order? There's no better time to get these things straightened out than now.

Writing a novel is full of tasks both large and small, from figuring out the whole freaking plot to making sure that the paragraphs are aligned properly. Tackling one of the smaller tasks still gets you closer to the finish line, and sometimes it can help you get your rhythm back.

BE PATIENT

It's important to know that your first day back after a long absence will not be as productive as a normal day. This is okay. Knowing is the first step in not panicking and not getting down on yourself. Don't set page goals, and don't kick yourself when you try to spend a day writing and get extremely little done. Just focus on getting your rhythm back. That's all you need to accomplish.

It's going to be a slow and likely unproductive day, but even a subpar day is helpful because it's getting you back into the flow. Even a marginal day gets you closer to finishing.

And then, after you struggle through that day and you've gotten back in the saddle, it's crucially important to . . .

FOLLOW UP A GOOD DAY OF WRITING WITH ANOTHER DAY OF WRITING

You slogged your way back into a writing rhythm. Don't waste it!

Chase it as quickly as possible with a good, solid, uninterrupted, and productive chunk of time. Now you have momentum. So keep it up!

The second day will remind you of what it feels like to be in a writing groove, and every day after that will be much easier.

Also, shouting "I'm back, baby!!" to no one in particular is strongly encouraged.

Rule #34
YOU DON'T HAVE "WRITER'S BLOCK"

The most important thing you need to know about writer's block is this: it doesn't exist.

Seriously. Writer's block does not exist. It is not a worm that suddenly lodges itself in your brain, it is not a mysterious goblin that sneaks up on you and poisons you with an anti-writing serum, and it is not something that you need to fear coming down with.

Now, when I say writer's block doesn't exist, I don't mean that you will never have the feeling associated with writer's block or that people who say they have writer's block are big fakers. I've felt the feeling! I've been there.

But when people encounter the phenomenon otherwise known as "writer's block," what they are really describing is one thing and one thing only: writing stopped being fun.

That's it. That's all it means. The writing process stopped being easy and the words were no longer flowing as readily as they were in the beginning. Writing, in other words, just got really, ridiculously hard.

Writer's block is what happens when novels stop being polite and start getting real. The Real World: Writing!

But remember: it's a feeling. It is not something that will stop you from finishing, nor is it something that you have to give into because it's inevitable. You can't treat it like a virus that will pass in time if you just wait it out. You must seek a cure.

There are ways of dealing with "writer's block," and they all have one thing in common: work. Here are the strategies that will help:

FIGURE OUT THE PROBLEM YOU NEED TO SOLVE

Chances are you will, at some point, feel completely and utterly stuck. This isn't writer's block (which, again, doesn't exist). You're just stuck.

It's completely frustrating. And this is okay. There are going to be setbacks. Don't stress yourself out thinking that everything should always be easy.

Instead of focusing on your exasperation with your own writing abilities, it's eminently important to figure out *why* you're stuck. Does something in particular need to happen in your story that is stymieing you? Do you need to figure out how characters get from Point A to Point B? Is something just not feeling right, and so you need to go back and fix some things leading up to the sticky spot? Has a plot thread gone astray?

The first step to getting unstuck is understanding the problem you need to solve. Once you've identified the main issue, the solution is just around the corner. You might not know what to do immediately, and your brain might need to work itself toward the solution, but knowing the problem is a crucial nudge toward writing again.

GO OUTSIDE AND GET SOME FRESH AIR AND SUNSHINE

Once you have a general sense of the problem at hand and what you need to accomplish, it's okay to take a break. Give your brain a breather, get some Vitamin D, stare at some flowers, and ponder how in the world you ended up writing a novel and how maybe it would've been simpler to take up gardening instead.

Changing your location and experiencing some peace and quiet can help dislodge the clog in your brain. Find as much nature as you can, depending on where you live. Trees and grass and oxygen are magic.

EXERCISE

Get the blood flowing. Lift some weights. Punch a punching bag. Really punch that bag stupid novel argh *#&%@.

You'll be amazed at the ideas you'll have while exercising.

And not only this, but, as I'm sure you know, the brain is part of the body, so you might want to keep the whole enterprise healthy. You'll be happier and more creative if you spend time getting your heart rate up.

Whenever I was stuck with the *Jacob Wonderbar* series, I headed straight to the gym. The problems had often been solved by the time I got back to my apartment.

FORCE YOURSELF TO STARE AT A BLANK SCREEN UNTIL YOU THINK OF SOMETHING

This is the ripping-the-bandaid-off approach to dealing with writer's block. It is painful but utterly effective.

Turn off your Internet connection and cell phone. Close the blinds. Hide the TV remote. Lock the doors.

Open up your novel. And stare stare stare at the blinking cursor.

This is my absolute favorite technique for dealing with the affliction formerly known as writer's block. You just power through.

It is absolutely agonizing to stare at a blank screen and a blinking cursor. It can inspire feelings of panic and despair. You may start wondering if you'll ever think of another idea again. You may start to wonder if the blinking cursor was originally invented as a torture device.

But then, after ten minutes or more of staring at the blinking cursor of death, you'll eventually start to calm down. You'll do the only thing you can do in a quiet, Internet-less room with nothing else to occupy your attention: you will start thinking of ideas. If you concentrate and don't let the feeling overpower you, you'll eventually come up with something that will get you out of the writing block hole.

It may take minutes, or it may take hours. It may be the most agonizing few hours of your creative life, or you may be surprised at how quickly you get going.

But here's what happens after you've overcome your blockage and you get back into the flow: you'll be so euphoric that you're back on track that it will start feeling fun again.

You'll realize that the whole writing block thing never existed in the first place.

This next chapter will also help . . .

Rule #35

REMEMBER THE SOLUTION TO EVERY WRITING PROBLEM THAT HAS EVER EXISTED

Keep writing.

Rule #36
DREAM BIG, BUT BE REALISTIC

Even if you manage to skirt around the artist formerly known as writers' block, after the halfway point in writing a novel, it will no longer be easy. The initial heady buzz wore off long ago and the middle stretch is frighteningly complicated to write because you have so many plates spinning; it's extremely difficult to plan where to go next, the end is nowhere near, and you may be turning to daydreams to help make the amount of time and energy you're expending on your novel seem worth it.

You know these daydreams: your book is published and becomes the toast of the world, you have tea with Prince William and Kate Middleton, and you can't get a word in because they can't stop talking about how much they love your book and especially about how much they love *you*, you incredible genius you.

Or something like this. As previously recounted in Rule #31, these daydreams can be healthy and even helpful. They can be a very juicy carrot at the end of a 200-page long stick.

Just be careful.

There's a famous psychological study that shows that people who win the lottery and that people who are involved in catastrophic accidents return to the same original base level of happiness after two years. There's another one that says that people who make more than $75,000 a year aren't made much happier by further raises.

In other words, success and fortune are normative. When we experience success, no matter how great, we first experience a blip of happiness. Then we get used to it and start looking for what's around the bend.

For writers, this leads to the "If only" game.

You know how it goes: "If only I could finish my novel, then I'd be happy." Then you finish, and it's "If only I could find an agent, then I'd be happy." When you get an agent, it becomes "If only I could find a publisher, then I'd be happy. If only I could make the bestseller list, then I'd be happy. If only I could have as many Twitter followers as Neil Gaiman, then I'd be happy."

We allow our success to become the new normal, and we aren't satisfied for long. Then we work that much harder to get to the next level, and even when we reach that next milestone, we get used to it and look for what's next, because there's always another milestone to reach no matter how successful you are.

The daydreams you use to get through the tough times can become an "If only" milestone before you know it.

Writing is difficult, you don't always want to do it, and you're putting in such incredible hard work that your mind starts to drift to your book being published and taking off and becoming a bestseller and being the next *Harry Potter* (only more popular—we're all J.K. Rowlings before publication) and sitting on Oprah's couch (she brought the show back just for you!) and funding the construction of a levitating castle in the sky because you'll be rich enough.

You use these dreams to power through the difficult stretches and redouble your efforts. Again, this is perfectly natural. No judging. But these dreams are sort of like the dark side of the Force. Use them too much and you'll turn into a Sith Lord.

When you allow daydreams to fill the gap and get you through the tough times, or even when you just let your imagination get the best of you, the dreams can gradually evolve into the *reason* you were writing. At first they were helping you get through some tough stretches, but if you rely on them too much, they can gradually begin to feel like the reason you were doing it in the first place. You start thinking, if this dream doesn't come true, what were all those hours for? Why am I dealing with this frustration and pain if it's not going to amount to anything? Why am I doing this if it is not going to result in success beyond my wildest expectations?

The dreams start to become a crutch, and when that crutch inevitably disappears, you will fall over because you will have been leaning on an endlessly elusive dream.

It doesn't feel worth it anymore, even if you've achieved the type of success for which you *should* be extremely proud and that would have made you happy if your expectations had been kept in check. If you don't rely on daydreams, the modest or even huge successes you experience will feel satisfying instead of vaguely disappointing. If you keep your wits, you will be able to recognize your grand achievements when they actually happen. (This sounds easy, but it's actually harder than you might think.)

So, be careful with those dreams. They seem bright and shiny and harmless, they can help you through the tough times, and it's fun to let your imagination run wild for a little while, but if you let them get the best of you, you'll eventually hollow out and get all wrinkly and lightning will start shooting from your fingertips, at least until Darth Vader throws you into the reactor core.

BALANCE YOUR CONFIDENCE AND SELF-DOUBT

Writers have a pretty unique challenge.

On the one hand, you have to have the confidence to spend hours and hours at something without really knowing how it's going to turn out, and often without knowing whether you actually have the talent or the right idea to create a story that people will love. It takes fortitude, commitment, and deep confidence that what you're doing is worth it.

On the other hand, if you are going to have the ability to make your work better, you need to have enough self-doubt to be critical of it. You have to turn a relatively cold eye to your writing to spot its flaws and weak spots, you have to be self-aware enough to know your own weaknesses, and you have to be dedicated enough to improve your flaws and not get carried away with self-indulgent writing.

These impulses, of self-confidence and self-doubt, seem contradictory, but I'd argue that they are two sides of the same coin. It's all confidence.

To be able to spot your own flaws requires confidence. Staring your own weaknesses and flaws in the face doesn't come from a place of self-doubt, but from a place of strength. You have to be a strong person in order to own up to your own flaws and to shoulder the responsibility of making your work better.

There are some writers out there who seem boldly confident and brash, but it's really a mask. When someone suffers from supreme overconfidence and can't see their own flaws, in truth they're not confident at all. They lack the strength to admit their own shortcomings. We all have flaws, but not everyone has the strength to overcome them.

On the flip side, it's also important not to overdo the self-doubt and paralyze yourself with indecision. It's easy to despair and feel that you're not good enough and that you'll never get there, which leads you to magnify the weaknesses in your writing, especially when you're just beginning. This, too, is what happens when you are approaching writing with insufficient confidence.

The only way to strike the right balance as a writer is to build up your confidence in a healthy, clear-headed way.

Confidence will give you the strength to doubt yourself. Don't be down on yourself for being down on yourself.

I once attended a retreat where I heard a talk from Ben Silbermann, the co-founder and CEO of Pinterest. He talked about a journey that I think would be extremely familiar to any novelist. He embarked on many false starts after he quit his job at Google, building several semi-successful sites, before finally arriving at one of the most influential designs of our time: Pinterest. During his talk, he mentioned that even after all his success with Pinterest, he still lived at the intersection of terror and joy.

This is exactly how you have to live as a writer. You have to be strong enough to put yourself out there and brave and confident enough to share a part of yourself with the world. You do it because you love it so much that you're willing to risk everything negative that can possibly come your way.

You also have to be self-critical enough to edit your work, and you have to fear failure and worry that your best might not be good enough, which can push you just that much further. You have to be scared of what will happen if you don't do your best. You can never get comfortable.

Terror and joy. Confidence and self-doubt. The best artists live in the uncomfortable middle.

Rule #38
EDIT AS YOU GO

The first step in the editing process actually begins before you finish your first draft. So, uh, I hope you read this before you finish your first draft.

This crucial initial pass is self-editing as you go.

As you're writing a novel, there is always the temptation to just power through and get something, anything, on the page so that you can just finish the writing-the-novel part, trusting that you're going to go back and revise it later. However, I believe it is highly beneficial to engage in some self-editing along the way.

Some people feel like they need to flip the self-editing switch off because it's easy to fall into a state of paralysis, where you are trying to write a polished final draft on the very first try. Some people find it horrifying to quickly revisit something they've already slaved over. They feel crippled by their critical eye, and sometimes letting go and just allowing the words to flow without thinking about them too heavily can be freeing. These writers may just charge forward without looking back.

But abandon all hope ye who forgo self-editing entirely. There is one very simple and important reason why you should self-edit: problems can snowball.

A weak spot that you brush over in the first few chapters can progress from there and worm its way through the novel in such a way that it can become very, very difficult to fix later on. When something happens near the beginning of your novel that just doesn't work, it can be extremely tricky to change it and still make the rest of the novel make sense. You've built a house on a shaky foundation, and changing this may require you to tear things down to the studs. For example, if a character actually needs to die in Chapter 3, it can be extremely, extremely challenging to disentangle that character from a plot in which they currently survive until the climax.

A further challenge is that self-editing is not as easy as it sounds. It's very difficult to be a fully self-aware writer and spot your own flaws, especially if you're knee-deep in writing the novel and squarely in the "I have no idea if any of this is any good" stage of the process, which, by the way, is the stage you're in 99% of the time that you spend writing a novel.

But it's crucial to stop, think, and try to imagine yourself as a reader, as well as remember the writing advice you know, and ask yourself very honestly: "Is this working?"

Chances are, even when you're in the throes of that initial burst of confidence, you'll know when something isn't working. There will be a quiet, tiny, nagging voice that you won't be able to shut off as long as you're listening to it. This voice usually manifests itself as a sneaking suspicion that you have somehow gone astray, even if you can't pinpoint the exact moment when it happened.

Listen to The Voice, which speaks quietly and almost imperceptibly. The Voice sounds way more like "Um . . . psst. Oh God, I'm *so* sorry to bug you, you seem like you're having so much fun, but, um, are you really sure about cow aliens?" than "Duh! Wake up! This is wrong!"

The Voice is not assertive, it will not demand to be heard, but it is extremely useful if you can tune into it. And you can only hear it if you stop and put your ears to the train tracks to listen from time to time.

If you practice self-editing as you go, you will save yourself a great deal of editing when you're finished.

Still, this is only a partial time-saver, because everyone, and I mean everyone, has work to do when they're done writing. There is no such thing as a perfect first draft.

So just know that even if you've self-edited, you'll still have more editing to do. Never lull yourself into feeling like you're close to being "finished" as you approach the end of your first draft.

Novels are made and broken by the editing process. Be ready for it. But you'll lessen the blow if you have listened to The Voice along the way.

REVISING

Rule #39
TAKE TIME TO CELEBRATE

You have completed a first draft.

Congrats! Give yourself a round of applause. You are a freaking champion: 99.9% of everyone who has ever lived in the world wanted to write a novel (note: I made this statistic up), but the vast majority never got around to it. Most of the ones who started never finished. You are not one of these people.

You've done it. You are officially a person who has written a novel. No one can take this away from you. No one. You did it. No one can ever accuse you of not going after your dreams. You should feel proud. It took a ton of time, hardship, and creative energy, but you did it. You have set out on a monumental task, and you have come away with 150 to 250 (or however many) pages of your soul spilled out onto paper.

As I'm writing a novel, when times are tough and I'm exhausted and I need some extra motivation, I like to let my mind wander to the reward I will give myself when I finish my first draft. And when I finish, I actually go and do these things. Sometimes I'll let myself play a computer game (Crazytown!), or I'll buy a fancy bottle of wine or go out for a nice dinner. I let myself have the free time to do some of the things I don't normally do because I'm a writer with a full-time job who doesn't have time for normal hobbies.

So when you finish that novel, let yourself celebrate! Take a little bit of time off. Not only do you deserve it, you'll need to get some distance from your novel before you can come back to it anyway, so take a few weeks to let your head clear and enjoy some of the things you missed out on as you were diligently chipping away at the huge, huge, HUGE task that you have now accomplished, being the good and diligent and hard-working writer that you are.

Let's review: You. Wrote. A. Novel.

You. You did it. Enjoy it. Go do something fun.

Then, once you're done celebrating and have given yourself some time and distance, it's time to get back to work. Because your first draft probably sucks.

Rule #40:
REVISING IS JUST AS IMPORTANT AS WRITING

Here's how to start revising your novel after you've finished your first draft: read your book.

It sounds simple. It is not. Because as you're re-reading your book, you have to shake the tendency to read uncritically.

Provided you have let some time pass before you revisit your book (which, by the way, you should), once you return to it, you may be struck by your own ingenuity as you re-encounter parts you forgot you wrote. You will be lulled into speed-reading a narrative that you have memorized by heart. You may crack yourself up with your own hilariousness and wonder how it is that everyone in the world is so lucky as to live at this time in which you are the bard of your era.

All of this is great, but it's not going to help you to be a good reviser.

In order to shake yourself out of auto-read mode, you have to slow down. You have to think. You have to take in your novel as if you have not actually read it a thousand times before and know exactly what is going to happen, because, you know, you really have read it a thousand times before and know exactly what is going to happen. You have to be very, very self-critical.

One helpful trick for shaking yourself out of auto-read mode is to put yourself in the shoes of someone else reading your novel. Pick someone you know extremely well, and whose response you can imagine in any given situation, such as your mom or your significant other or your kid sister, and try to read the novel through his or her eyes. What would they think of the part where the charming rogue fights the peacock? Would they be fooled when the villain reveals himself to be a malevolent mold spore?

This mental distancing will help you spot problems and see your novel as someone else would see it. The extra mental gymnastics necessary for reading this way will slow you down, and you'll trick yourself into reading critically. Don't be freaked out by your family's imaginary responses when you get to the dark scenes and saucy romantic encounters, but do try to take into account the varied responses to the more mundane moments, and use these as a way to spot problems or weaknesses.

Then, when you find things you want to change, avoid the temptation of diving right in. Don't get lost in trying to make revisions right away. Instead, as you read, take note of the changes you want to make until you've gone through the entire book. Think of it as a pre-surgical checkup. You need to assess the patient very thoroughly before you begin open-heart surgery. Do your triage before you operate.

Once you've re-read your novel a few times (yes, read it through more than once) and you've taken note of everything that needs fixing, you're ready to begin your novel's surgery. But be very, very systematic about how you go about it.

Confronting a revision can be extremely daunting because of the Cascade Effect: when you change one plot point, it often necessitates two more changes to ensure that the plot still makes sense after the change, which prompts still more changes, and more, and more. Ten or more changes can cascade from a single change, even a minor one, particularly when the change is near the beginning and it requires you to eliminate a character or make events unfold in an entirely new way.

In order to avoid Cascade Effect Terror, I find that it's helpful to work on only one plot change at a time, starting with the most massive changes and working down to the smallest.

Here's why you should start with the big changes before you tackle the small ones: it's a waste of time to make small changes that will only be swallowed up over the course of a much larger revision. It's not helpful to fine tune the dialogue in a chapter you're going to cut entirely because the whole plotline no longer makes sense.

If you approach changes by starting with the most important and far-reaching and moving to the smallest and least important, you'll be as efficient in your revisions as possible. Don't get distracted by the smaller things that bother you about the book as you're making the big changes. Just make that big change, and then all the other changes that become necessary once you've eliminated a character or altered a major plot point.

Then, once everything makes sense, move on to the next most important change, then the one after that, etc.

When you're done fixing the main plot points, you can move on to the chapters, refining how these unfold, and then move on to the line edits and minor tweaks.

Eventually, when the plot is in order, you'll drill down to the level of your prose. When you do, it's in-credibly important to be aware of your tendencies and weaknesses. If you write in an overly spare fashion, you may need to layer in description to ground the reader and flesh things out. If you're overly verbose, you may need to pare back, clarify, and look for ways to make scenes more readable.

Above all, know your writerly tics. My biggest personal tic: characters looking at things. Jacob saw such and such, Sarah looked at Jacob, Jacob looked down, Sarah glanced at the ceiling, Dexter stared at his shoes, and the reader rolled their eyes and stared into space because they got tired of all the characters looking at things. I always have to find ways to vary the gestures and the descriptions so that my novels aren't an endless series of glances.

Other writers insert too many interjections at the beginning of sentences, "Okay, so I probably didn't need that 'okay, so' at the beginning of this sentence." "I mean, I'm probably saying 'I mean' too much." Other writers have their characters sigh too much.

When you're successful at stepping back from your work, not only will your writing tics be glaringly apparent, they will also drive you insane. This is a good thing.

If, after tackling all the changes (both major and minor), you've revised your book as far as you can on your own, and you can't think of anything else you need to change . . .

You're still not done.

Rule #41
COMPLETE THE REVISION CHECKLIST

- Is the main plot arc initiated close enough to the beginning of the novel that you won't lose the reader?
- Does your protagonist alternate between up and down moments, with the most intense toward the end?
- Are you able to trace the major plot arcs throughout the book? Do they have up and down moments?
- Do you have enough conflict?
- Does the reader see both the best and worst characteristics of your main characters?
- Do your characters have backstories and histories? Do these impact the plot?
- Is the pacing correct for your genre? Is it consistent?
- Is your voice consistent? Is it overly chatty, overly sarcastic, or overly anything?

- Is the description sufficient at grounding the reader in the characters' world?
- Is there *too much* description?
- Does change happen in the world of your novel? Do you know how this change impacts your characters?
- Are there lulls in the plot that will lose the reader? Are there stretches where you risk exhausting the reader with nonstop action?
- Are momentous events given the weight they deserve?
- Look closely at each chapter. If you can take out a chapter and the plot still makes sense, is the chapter really necessary? Should some events be folded in with others?
- Look closely at each character. If you can take out a character and the plot still makes sense, is the character really necessary? Should some characters be folded in with others?
- Do the relationships between your characters develop, change, and become more complicated as the book goes on?
- What do your characters want? Is it apparent to the reader? Do they have both conscious and unconscious motivations?
- Do you know your writing tics? Do you overuse adverbs, metaphors, facial expressions, non-"said" dialogue tags, or interjections? Have you removed them?

- Do you overuse certain words or phrases?
- Does your book come to a completely satisfying conclusion? Does it feel rushed?
- Do your main characters emerge from the book irrevocably changed?
- Do each of your scenes make dramatic sense on their own and move the overall plot forward?
- Do you have any nagging doubts about your novel? What are they, and can you fix them?

Rule #42
FIND SOMEONE OBJECTIVE TO EDIT YOUR WORK

There will come a point in the self-editing process where you've gone as far as you possibly can on your own. The chances are that by this point you'll be cross-eyed and hate everything to do with your novel, including the air that surrounds it and the space in between the words on the page. Now it's time to seek feedback from the outside world.

This could mean a significant other (be careful, though!), a critique partner, a friend, a mortal enemy . . . but someone.

How to find this person? Well, this will partly be driven by who is willing. This is why friends can be helpful, even though you risk taking their criticism more personally than you might a stranger's, and even though they risk letting their perception of you and affection for you shape their reading. At the very least, they may feel obligated to help you out at a time when you desperately need it, because that's what friends are for.

But beware: friends and loved ones can't always be counted on for objective advice. They may wish to please you and may tell you they love your work even if that's not actually the case. You may be better off seeking advice elsewhere.

Another place you can seek feedback is from a critique group, whether in your local area or online. This will require some reciprocity on your part, because you will likely have to give good feedback in order to get good feedback.

If you don't have someone readily available and need a critique relatively quickly, or if you would like some input from someone who has worked in the business, then it's time to consider a freelance editor. There are some wildly talented editors out there who can help authors with their manuscripts for a fee. This can be a very positive route to take.

However, before you mortgage the farm to pay a freelance editor, keep the following in mind:

DON'T SPEND MONEY THAT YOU CAN'T AFFORD TO LOSE

If it feels like too much money, it is definitely too much money.

Feedback is helpful, but not at the expense of funds that could be better used elsewhere. If you can spare it and it won't hurt a whit, go for it. Otherwise, there are plenty of free ways to get good feedback, such as the aforementioned method of connecting with a critique partner online or joining a local writing group.

No revision is worth bankrupting yourself.

CHECK THE EDITOR'S CREDENTIALS AND WATCH OUT FOR SCAMS

Find out what his or her experience is, who they've worked with in the past, and whether the amount they are charging is commensurate with their experience. Do your research and only work with an editor with whom you are completely comfortable.

There are quite a few unscrupulous and fake agents and editors out there. Google the person you're thinking of working with, and, again, check their credentials.

Beware of anyone over-promising on what they can really deliver.

BEAR IN MIND THAT THE MERE FACT THAT YOU'VE WORKED WITH AN EDITOR IS PROBABLY NOT GOING TO BOOST YOUR CHANCES WITH AN AGENT

Some agents feel that it is a benefit that an author has worked with an editor. When I was an agent, it didn't mean that much to me. I assumed that authors received good feedback and worked to make their manuscripts better. Whether the feedback came from a friend or a paid editor wasn't important to me. I don't think you get a bonus because you paid for it.

AGENTS DON'T CARE ABOUT TYPOS (WITHIN REASON)

Copyediting is not particularly necessary prior to submitting to agents. Barring a significant learning disability that interferes with the basic readability of your manuscript, your own grammar and spell-check-assisted spelling skills should be sufficient to ensure that your manuscript has only the occasional typo, which an agent will not worry about.

DO NOT LET AN EDITOR SUBMIT TO AGENTS ON YOUR BEHALF

This is getting a little ahead of things, but when the time comes and your manuscript is truly finished, I wouldn't advise letting editors submit on your behalf. Agents usually want to hear directly from the authors they're potentially going to be working with. A good editor may absolutely have contacts in the business they could refer you to, but you should still be the person who communicates with the agent.

KNOW WHAT YOU'RE PAYING FOR

Make sure you have a very clear understanding up front of what you're paying for and what you'll be receiving. Make sure you and the editor have a clear understanding about what you're hoping to get out of the edit.

And make sure you're communicating well.

THERE'S NO MAGIC BULLET

Keep your expectations in check. The editor is helping you with your manuscript. It's up to you to make the changes, and their help is no guarantee that your project will find representation or publication. The goal is to help you improve your manuscript, but the final state of the novel is ultimately your responsibility.

Basically, it all comes down to this: do your research and keep your eyes open, but don't be overly paranoid. There are freelance editors out there who provide a valuable service, and assuming you find the right match, their feedback can be of real help as you plug onward to representation.

Remember, though, that an editor is not essential. You just need good feedback from whatever source can provide it.

The advice that comes back to you should be positive, useful, strike you with the occasional "Why didn't I see that?!" moment, and, perhaps most importantly, be consistent with your vision for the project. In other words, the critiquer shouldn't simply be telling you how *they* would have written it.

Once you have received this advice . . .

Rule #43
ACCEPT FEEDBACK GRACIOUSLY AND WITH AN OPEN MIND

If you will pardon the metaphor, receiving a manuscript critique is kind of like having a colonoscopy. Even when the prognosis is good, the procedure is invasive and unsettling.

Having your work critiqued is not. fun. at. all. The very thing that you most want to happen ("Oh my God, I love it, don't change a thing, you are a certifiable genius!!") is also the least helpful.

When you receive a critique, your soul is lying on the table, exposed. And your time. And your dreams.

And yet how you respond to the feedback is everything. If you're good at incorporating suggestions, your manuscript is going to be vastly better. If you're bad at it, you've wasted your critique partner's time as well as your own.

So how do you go about this painful but vital process? Here's what to do:

WHEN YOU GET YOUR EDITORIAL LETTER/CRITIQUE, STEEL YOUR RESOLVE, READ IT ONCE, PUT IT AWAY, AND DON'T THINK ABOUT IT OR ACT ON IT FOR AT LEAST A COUPLE OF DAYS.

Treat an editorial letter as if it's a radioactive substance that you need to become gradually acclimated to over the course of several days. It needs to be absorbed in small doses, kept at arm's length, and quarantined when necessary, at least until you are able to overcome the dangerous side effects that can accompany reading an editorial letter: anger, paranoia, excessive pride, delusions of grandeur, and/or homicidal tendencies.

Should you find yourself experiencing any of these side effects, consult your writing support group immediately for an antidote.

It's hard to have your work critiqued, and it's tempting to take it personally. Just know that it's a normal reaction, and in a couple of days you'll feel better. Once you've calmed down and can consider the changes without your heart racing, you know you're ready to start working. Try to remember your book is intended for the general reading public and that it's better to hear flaws now, before your work reaches a wider audience.

GO WITH YOUR GUT

You don't have to accept every single suggestion. In fact, you probably shouldn't accept every single suggestion. One of the most important skills you need as a writer is being good at determining which are the best recommendations. If you don't agree with a change, big or small, it's okay to stick to your guns if you feel you are justified in doing so.

Only make sure it's really your gut talking and not your lazy bone. Or your bull head. Or your stubborn foot (is that a thing?). If you are going to ignore a suggestion, you had better have a very, very good reason for it.

Often when you resist a suggestion, it is because fixing the problem that the person has cited would be very, very hard. This isn't the right approach. You have to have the wisdom to accept criticism even (or especially) when it means a huge amount of work.

And on that note . . .

DON'T SIMPLY IGNORE THE SUGGESTIONS YOU DON'T AGREE WITH

Often when someone makes a specific suggestion for a change to a certain scene or plot line, you won't agree with it, and you'll throw up your hands and say that there's no way you're going to make that change.

But! Even if you don't agree with the specific remedy suggested by the editor, it's important to remember that *something* prompted them to suggest the change. And this something could be an underlying problem that needs to be addressed, even if you don't agree with the exact solution your editor/critique partner proposed.

Even if you don't agree with a particular suggestion, stop and think about why they suggested making the change. They didn't just recommend it for their own health. Chances are, you'll spot something that really is an issue; once you've identified the problem, you'll find your own way of dealing with it.

BE SYSTEMATIC

Here's how I go about tackling all the changes proposed in an editorial letter.

First, I color code the letter. I mark all the changes I'm definitely going to make in green, all the ones I don't plan to make in red (I try to make sure there is way more green than red), and mark the suggestions

I'm not sure about in yellow (these have a tendency to turn green). Then I have a nice color-coded editorial letter and the beginnings of an action plan.

After this, I engage in the triage process described in Rule #40, starting with the most significant changes and working down from there to the smallest line edits, on the grounds that it's kind of pointless to work on line edits first if the chapter is going to get deleted or if the small changes are going to be consumed by the bigger changes.

Once all the scenes are roughly in place, I move to the low-hanging fruit and start polishing on a scene-by-scene, and then line-by-line, level.

IF YOU FIND YOURSELF GETTING MAD, IT'S PROBABLY BECAUSE YOUR EDITOR/CRITIQUE PARTNER IS RIGHT

Great suggestions are easy to accept. You usually smack your head and think, "Why didn't I think of that?!"

Bad suggestions are easy to reject. You just think, "Naw, I'm not doing that."

I've found that when the suggestions make you mad, it's probably because the suggestions are correct. Your brain is just having trouble admitting it, usually because the changes are challenging to make or because you're overly wedded to that particular stretch of the novel.

If I'm mad, it's the absolute worst. I have way more work than I thought I had to do. But if I *don't* do it, my novel will suffer as a result. It means I have to do it.

So . . . I calm down and get back to work.

LISTEN, LISTEN, LISTEN, LISTEN, AND LISTEN TO YOUR EDITOR

Easy to say. Tough to practice.

Rule #44
EVEN WHEN YOU'RE FINISHED, YOU'RE NOT FINISHED

We have previously discussed the frustrating point in the writing process where you become utterly sick and tired of your book. It happens.

Now take that feeling, multiply it by infinity, and then double it again, and you will have a rough approximation of the loathing you will feel toward your novel, the entire writing process, words, and all the languages that have ever been invented as you go about the arduous task of revising your novel when you really just want to be finished already, dear God, when will it end?

This is normal. It's called revision fatigue.

The biggest obstacle that revision fatigue poses isn't even the fatigue itself, though that is substantial, but rather that the revision fatigue is accompanied by a feeling that your novel is a colossal, irredeemable mess and that you can't for the life of you figure out whether a single word of it is actually any good, let alone remember why you started writing it in the first place. When people ask you how your book is going, you frighten them with the depth of your hostility toward them for daring to ask about that nightmarish pile of crap otherwise known as your novel (never let it be said that it's easy to be friends with a writer).

The best and only way to deal with revision fatigue is to trust that the poisonous emotions stirring in your blackened heart are useful and necessary feelings. You have reached the ornery teenage years of the novel-writing process. Just as your belief in the insane alienhood of your parents gave you a healthy sense of wanting to move the heck away from home after high school, revision fatigue will give you the emotions you need at the exact moment you need them. Namely, it will allow you to let go of your affection for your book, which will allow you to tackle the big problems.

What better time to turn a truly critical eye on your book than when you think it is a disgusting affront to humanity? Lean into these feelings, use them well, and you'll be a better writer for it. Stew in revision fatigue and get mean with your book. Be ruthless. You'll be better able to spot what needs fixing, and you'll be more honest with yourself about the changes you need to make.

Despite the intensity of revision fatigue and the manner in which it turns writers into borderline psychopaths, there is another important silver lining: you're almost done. You really are close to the finish line. It's time to dig deep, keep that forward momentum going, and don't let your desire to be finished make you lose sight of how utterly necessary it is to make your work as good as possible and how much you'll eventually appreciate the fact that you slogged your way through.

You are at the point in the marathon where you can't feel your legs, and the only thing keeping you going is your momentum and the fact that the finish line is so close. (Or so I've heard. I would never do something as insane as running twenty-six miles in a single session. Or ever.)

The real danger is getting discouraged by your fatigue and just calling your work finished, turning it in before you've given yourself some time to utilize this fatigue. It can be demoralizing, after all that time and effort, to revisit your work and feel unsure of what it was all for, but you have to do it, and revision is one of the most important, if not *the* most important, parts of writing a novel. Revision is where good novels become great novels and where under-revised novels fail.

Just know that your revision fatigue will eventually pass. Let yourself simmer in it, power through, and keep working. Once you're done revising, you'll feel that overwhelming elation that everyone experiences when they cross the finish line of a marathon.

Well. People who run, anyway.

Rule #45
KNOW WHEN YOU'RE DONE

But, uh, how *do* you know when you're done?

It is quite possible to tinker with a book endlessly as a way to avoid facing the uncertainty and potential pain that inevitably stems from showing your work to strangers who might think you stink. You can fiddle with individual words, rewrite scenes until the horse has been beaten to death in various forms of the afterlife that humankind never knew existed, and you can come up with seventy-two alternate endings just to make sure the one you arrived at really is the best.

But at some point a novel has to be done.

There is only one way to know if a novel is done enough to move on to the next step, and that is by *deciding* that it's done after some honest self-reflection.

The self-reflection is very necessary, because if you are in the depths of revision fatigue, your entire being may well be shouting that it's doner than done. But if it's the revision fatigue talking, it's not the right decision. Or, if you are in the depths of submitmy-workophobia, you might be tinkering with the book just to tinker with it, even if the changes aren't making the book substantively better.

When deciding whether I'm actually done or not, I take a mental step back from the book. I take a deep breath. I take a bit of a break. I re-read the novel for the millionth time and make sure that, as I do so, I'm only fixing typos and making minor changes here and there, if I'm changing anything at all.

Then I ask myself these two questions:

AM I SATISFIED WITH HOW EVERYTHING FITS TOGETHER AND DOES EVERYTHING REALLY AND TRULY MAKE SENSE?

CAN I THINK OF ANYTHING ELSE I CAN POSSIBLY DO TO MAKE THE BOOK BETTER?

The answers should be "yes" and "no," if you're keeping score.

At some point, you'll run out of ideas. At some point, you'll re-read the novel and stop making changes. At some point, you'll just know you're done, and it won't be the revision fatigue talking, you will just really, truly, and actually be done. Or you'll realize the changes that you're making are kind of pointless and aren't going to make the difference between the success and failure of your book.

In which case . . .

Rule #46
GIVE YOURSELF A PAT ON THE BACK

You're done! You've done it! You're really, really done! Confetti should be falling from the ceiling, but it never actually does, so confetti of the imagination! You have written and, more importantly, revised a novel!

CONGRATULATIONS.

So. Um. Now what?

You'll have decisions to make ahead, including whether to self-publish or to start querying agents, as well as coming to grips with the nuts and bolts of getting a book published. But all this can wait for a moment. Instead, take a moment to congratulate yourself on an incredible accomplishment and to brace yourself for what's next. As difficult and patience-requiring as writing and revising are, the step that comes after you finish a novel requires still more patience. This is because success for writers, even if it arrives, does not tend to come quickly.

It seems like there are authors who come out of nowhere, get bazillion dollar book deals, make bazillions more dollars after the book comes out, and then ride off into the sunset of legends.

It's tempting to believe that all it takes to achieve meteoric success is a novel (yours, specifically), and then all the rest of that whole becoming-a-huge-success thing will just fall rapidly and effortlessly into place.

The truth is a lot more banal: success in all its forms takes a lot of work, a lot of patience, and a lot of luck.

There aren't any shortcuts in life, and least of all in writing. As you now know all too well, books don't just spring forth fully formed. Becoming a writer is a process and a journey, and it is the result of, at minimum, a lifetime of reading and a ton of work on craft, and it usually takes several tries before you get it right. Success is not something that falls from the sky, even if it looks from the outside as if it arrived instantaneously.

Every endeavor worth doing takes time, and so it is with achieving the success you want for your work. As patient and diligent as you've been throughout the writing process, try to keep your expectations in check, derive your satisfaction from the task you've just accomplished, and don't be lulled into thinking the next stage of the writing life will be any easier. It will absolutely be satisfying, but there's nothing easy about any of the stages, no matter how successful you become.

You may have finished a novel, but your journey as a writer is likely just starting. Wherever your journey with this particular novel takes you, keep on writing and keep on enjoying the writing life—no matter what happens.

Keep working on your craft. Keep improving. Keep persevering. Be patient.

If this book doesn't work out as you hope, write another one. And if that one doesn't work out, write another one. And if that one doesn't work out, write another one.

We each have our own journey. There's no single trajectory to success, and we're all the better for it. Rather than wishing for lightning to strike quickly, it's better to enjoy seeing it flash in the distance and know that your time will come.

But don't forget to give yourself a round of applause and throw some confetti in the air. You've earned it.

OBEY THE TEN COMMANDMENTS FOR THE HAPPY WRITER

Writers aren't generally known as the happiest lot. In case you think this is a new development, a letter surfaced that was written by Edgar Allen Poe to his editor in 1842, and in it he was apologizing for drinking too much and begging for money.

But believe it or not, writing and happiness can, in fact, go together. Here are ten ways for a writer to stay positive:

1) ENJOY THE PRESENT

Writers are dreamers, and dreamers tend to daydream about the future and concoct wildly optimistic scenarios that involve bestsellerdom, riches, and interviews with Ryan Seacrest. In doing so, they forget to enjoy the present. I call this the "If only" game, as previously discussed in Rule #36.

You know how it goes: "If only I could find an agent, *then* I'd be happy." When you get an agent, it then becomes: "If only I could get published, *then* I'd be happy." And so on.

The only way to stay sane in the writing business is to enjoy every step as you're actually experiencing it. Happiness is not around the bend. It's found in the present.

Because writing is pretty great; otherwise, why are you doing it?

2) MAINTAIN YOUR INTEGRITY

With frustration comes temptation. It's tempting to try and beat the system, whether that's by having someone else write your query, lying to the people you work with, or, you know, concocting the occasional fake memoir.

This may even work in the short term, but unless you are Satan incarnate (and I hope you're not), it will steadily chip away at your happiness and confidence, and your heart will shrivel and blacken into something that they show kids in health class to scare them away from smoking.

Don't do it.

3] RECOGNIZE THE FORCES THAT ARE OUTSIDE YOUR CONTROL

While it's tempting to think that it's your fault if your book doesn't sell, or that it's your agent's fault, the industry's fault, or the fault of a public that just doesn't recognize your genius, a lot of the time it's just luck not going your way.

Chance is *big* in the book business. Huge. Gambling has nothing on the incredibly delicate and complex calculus that results in a book taking off.

Bow before the whims of fate, because chance is more powerful than you and any agent combined.

4] DON'T NEGLECT YOUR FRIENDS AND FAMILY

No book is worth losing a friend, losing a spouse, or losing crucial time with your children. Hear me? *No* book is worth it. Not one. Not a bestseller, not a passion project, nothing.

Friends and family first. *Then* writing.

Writing is not an excuse to neglect your friends and family. Unless you don't like them very much.

5) DON'T QUIT YOUR DAY JOB

Quitting a job you need to pay the bills in order to write a novel is like selling your house and putting the proceeds into lottery tickets.

You don't have to quit your job in order to write. There is time in the day. You may have to sacrifice your relaxation time, your sleep time, or your reality television habit, but there is time. You just have to do it.

6) KEEP UP WITH THE PUBLISHING INDUSTRY NEWS

It may seem counterintuitive to follow the news of a business in which layoffs often constitute the bulk of the headlines, but it behooves you to keep yourself informed. You'll be happier (and more successful) if you know what you're doing. And agents and editors will appreciate your publishing savvy.

7) REACH OUT TO FELLOW WRITERS

No one knows how hard it is to write better than the people who have tried to do it themselves. Their company is golden.

Reach out and touch a writer. Plus, the Internet allows you to reach out to writers without smelling anyone's coffee breath.

8] PARK YOUR JEALOUSY AT THE DOOR

Writing can turn ordinary people into raving lunatics when they start to believe that another author's success is undeserved. Do not begrudge other writers their success.

Even if they suck.

9] BE THANKFUL FOR WHAT YOU HAVE

If you have time to write, you're doing pretty well. There are millions of starving people around the world, and they're not writing because they're starving. If you're writing, you're doing just fine. Appreciate it.

10] KEEP WRITING

Didn't find an agent? Keep writing.

Book didn't sell? Keep writing.

Book sold? Keep writing.

OMG an asteroid is going to crash into the planet and enshroud it in ten feet of ash? Keep writing. People will need something to read in the resulting permanent winter.

ACKNOWLEDGMENTS

Many of these rules were drawn from blog posts I've written over the years, and the entire guide would not be possible without everyone who has read my blog and contributed with their presence and astute comments, which taught me so much about the writing process. Thank you, everyone, and particularly to Nora Murad, Sara the Reluctant Yogi, and David Kazzie, who suggested topics I ended up incorporating into these 47 rules.

This guide benefitted immensely from the contributions of two fantastic editors, Christine Pride and Bryan Russell, who helped shape the concept and made me write the words better, from D. Robert Pease, who designed the interior, and from designer extraordinaire Mari Sheibley, who created the cover.

Thanks so much to author friends Jeff Abbott, Lauren Billings, Lisa Brackmann, James Dashner, Jennifer Hubbard, Tahereh Mafi, Sarah McCarry, Daniel Jose Older, and Ransom Riggs for their encouragement. I also have immense gratitude for my fantastic agent, Catherine Drayton, for being supportive of this enterprise from the start.

Lastly, no writer can write without the patience and understanding of their friends and family. Thanks to Mom, Dad, Darcie, Mike, Scott, Beth and Kevin, and to Egya Appiah, Justin Berkman, Holly Burns, Madissen De Turris, Ben Dreyfuss, Emily Dreyfuss, Sonia Gil, Dan Goldstein, Cheryl Holloway, Matt Lasner, Maggie Mason, Kim Samek, Sean Slinksy, Sharon Vaknin, and Alice Wang for their support on this project.

ABOUT THE AUTHOR

Nathan Bransford is the author of *Jacob Wonderbar and the Cosmic Space Kapow* (Dial, May 2011), *Jacob Wonderbar for President of the Universe* (Dial, April 2012) and *Jacob Wonderbar and the Interstellar Time Warp* (Dial, February 2013). He was formerly a literary agent with Curtis Brown Ltd. and blogs at http://nathanbransford.com. He lives in Brooklyn.

Made in the USA
Lexington, KY
10 March 2014